Information Management

Information and its management are central to modern society. Organizations—private and public, national and international—have recognized that information is a key resource and that its management is critical for success.

Existing books on information management focus on the abilities of computers to process data, the development of information systems, and the management of IT resources. They often start with the computer as a key issue. Although *Information Management* acknowledges the importance of computers and data communication, it starts from a deeper understanding of the concepts of information and knowledge, and on the basis of this understanding, derives methods to use computers effectively. This textbook provides graduates of any discipline with an understanding of the theory and practice that underpins information management, and introduces students to the concepts and applications of information management techniques in a variety of organizational contexts.

In giving students strong philosophical foundations, Fons Wijnhoven's book will prove to be an excellent primer in information management.

Fons Wijnhoven is Associate Professor of Knowledge Management and Information Systems at Twente University, The Netherlands.

Information Management

An informing approach

Fons Wijnhoven

Routledge
Taylor & Francis Group

LONDON AND NEW YORK

First published 2009
by Routledge
2 Park Square, Milton Park, Abingdon, Oxon OX14 4RN

Simultaneously published in the USA and Canada
by Routledge
270 Madison Ave, New York, NY 10016

*Routledge is an imprint of the Taylor & Francis Group,
an informa business*

© 2009 Fons Wijnhoven

Typeset in Sabon by GreenGate Publishing Services, Tonbridge, Kent
Printed and bound in Great Britain by TJ International Ltd, Padstow,
Cornwall

British Library Cataloguing in Publication Data
A catalogue record for this book is available from the British Library

Library of Congress Cataloguing in Publication Data
Wijnhoven, Fons.

Information management: an informing approach/
Fons Wijnhoven. – 1st ed.

p. cm.
Includes bibliographical references and index.
1. Database management. 2. Databases. 3. Information resources
management. I. Title.
QA76.9.D3W535 2009
005.74–dc22
2009010364

ISBN13: 978-0-415-55214-1 (hbk)
ISBN13: 978-0-415-55215-8 (pbk)
ISBN13: 978-0-203-87069-3 (ebk)

ISBN10: 0-415-55214-1 (hbk)
ISBN10: 0-415-55215-X (pbk)
ISBN10: 0-203-87069-7 (ebk)

Contents

Figures

Tables

Foreword

When I took my first required macroeconomics class at the University of Texas at Austin decades ago, we were required to read Robert Heilbroner's bestselling book *The Worldly Philosophers: The Lives, Times and Ideas of the Great Economic Thinkers*. I was inspired by the intellectual contributions of great thinkers such as Adam Smith, Parson Thomas Malthus, David Ricardo, Karl Marx, Thorstein Veblen, John Maynard Keynes, and many others. It was very illuminating to see that current economic thought "stood on the shoulders of giants," many of whom wrote so many years ago. This background of economic philosophy has served me well over my entire career.

It is very appropriate that a textbook on information management be organized around C. West Churchman's book on inquiring systems. Inquiry is an activity that produces knowledge; hence, inquiring systems are designed to produce knowledge with the help of computers. This is the question to which Churchman's work is addressed: how to design computer systems (in an abstract sense) that can help produce knowledge. In exploring this question, he analyzes the epistemologies of four classic philosophers—Leibniz, Locke, Kant, and Hegel—and of Edgar A. Singer, one of his mentors. But to Churchman and the philosophers he cites, knowledge is a very special thing. Knowledge is only worthwhile if it can be used to help better the human condition. There is a strong ethical and moral component in Churchmanian knowledge.

Churchman's students Richard O. Mason and Ian I. Mitroff brought their mentor's ideas on inquiring systems theory into the information systems field early on with their landmark article in the journal *Management Science* in 1973. For all practical purposes this paper made inquiring systems theory basic to the field of information management. That Churchman was one of the first four people honored with the prestigious LEO Award in its inaugural year of 1999 attests to the importance that information systems scholars hold for his work. Mason himself was later named a LEO Award winner at least in part for continuing Churchman's work.

I think it is a brilliant idea to follow Kolb's model of learning by studying abstract philosophical concepts, experimenting with those concepts by applying them to concrete experiences, and reflecting on what has been learned. This is exactly the kind of approach that Churchman would have loved. If the abstract concepts seem difficult to grasp at first, do not despair. Churchman also wrote that "confusion is the essence of learning." This means that you have to be a little confused at first; then with experimentation and reflection, you will finally come to know. It may not be easy, but is well worth the effort in the long run.

Despite the fact that Churchman's work has been so influential in information systems scholarship, it has scarcely made its way into textbooks in the field. Other disciplines organize their texts around theories that ground the field, such as evolution in biology or relativity theory in physics. It is high time for an information management text to introduce students to some of the theories that ground scholarship in our field. This is the first textbook that I am aware of that is grounded in the fundamental philosophy of information management. It is long overdue, and I hope that it will inspire the students who study it for the remainder of their careers.

Jim Courtney
MIS Department
University of Central Florida
Orlando

Preface

This book is the result of an effort to develop a course on information management from a *non-technical* perspective especially for social science-oriented undergraduate programs. Given the current developments of information technology and the importance of information technology for everyday information management, this sounds almost a contradiction. One may ask: "How can we discuss something which is so much driven by technology from a human and social perspective?" The answer to this dilemma has been found in regarding information management as inherent to human life and social reality. Therefore, information management is as old as mankind, and one of the very first academic disciplines that developed in the arts of writing, speech, bureaucratic administration, philosophy, politics and management. This fact provides the key to the core idea behind this book: discussions of human information management from classic but still relevant traditions in the philosophy of knowing, i.e. epistemologies, as described by philosophers John Locke (1632–1704), Gottfried Wilhelm Leibniz (1646–1716), Immanuel Kant (1724–1804), and Georg Hegel (1770–1831). These philosophies have been very well summarized by C. W. Churchman, who integrated these perspectives on knowing in the pragmatist view of Edgar Singer (1873–1954).

Despite all the wisdom of these old philosophers, there are a few limitations to what they have given us. Three of these limitations are discussed in this book. The *first limitation* is that all the good ideas delivered by the philosophers we will discuss have been popular and were codified an age or more ago. Times have changed, and nowadays information technologies are provided, which ease data collection and handling, modeling and calculations, process and organization management, and communication over the globe in unprecedented ways. One could question if old philosophical insights, therefore, have become obsolete. The answer of this book is "absolutely not," and we can use good philosophical understandings to know more precisely what information and informing entail, so that we can make better and smarter uses of the technologies available. The problem, though, is that the worlds of information technology and epistemology do not meet frequently, which results in an underutilization of the opportunities information technology offers. This book will overcome this by offering concrete methods for bridging the gap between the type of knowledge people need and the opportunities of using information technology for informing.

The *second limitation* to be discussed in this book is that classic philosophers treat epistemology as a personal human effort, but mostly information management is an organizational process; so we will have to discuss information management in organizational contexts as well (see Chapter 6).

The *third limitation* is that these philosophers are brilliant in constructing overly complex arguments, but they do not always help non-philosophically trained people to understand the implications of their *abstract* thoughts in a practical way. I follow Kolb's (1984) theory on experiential learning to solve this problem, by letting the reader *experience* the implications of abstract notions by the description of methods and practices of information management in the information age. Additionally, I give the reader some time for *reflection* by providing "reflective practice" notes at the end of each chapter and references to additional readings. I have not based this text on original texts of these philosophers, which may be useful to improve a deeper philosophical insight (I leave this to philosophers of information), but have mainly used Churchman's, Mason and Mitroff's, and Courtney's interpretations to improve information management insights.

Although this book has been developed as a textbook for undergraduate social science and information science students, it has been written so that anyone with an interest in philosophy and the nature of information, and those who use IT intensively for informing, may find useful insights in this book. By adding more fundamental philosophical and information management methodological articles (suggested in the further reading suggestions at the end of each chapter), this book also may serve as a capstone for a foundations course on management and information systems for master's and PhD students.

Acknowledgments

This book is the result of building on the "shoulders of giants" in several ways:

- The basic idea of using philosophical epistemologies for explaining modes of information management is rooted in Mason and Mitroff (1973), who base their understanding on the work of Churchman (1971).
- The organizational extensions of these ideas are based on Courtney (2001) and related literature in information systems and organizations.
- Chapter 2 has made extensive use of Kroenke's very clear description of databases and MS-Access.
- Not being a philosopher myself, the descriptions of philosophers in Chapters 2, 3, 4, and 5 have been taken from relevant articles in the Stanford Encyclopedia of Philosophy, Churchman (1971), and Mason and Mitroff's (1973) discussion of the implications of Churchman's work for the information systems field. These descriptions have been commented on and placed in the context of organizations and twenty-first-century information management by myself.
- Chapter 3 has been partially written by my colleague Björn Kijl. Björn also has been a support through his encouragements from the beginning.
- Chapter 5 has been partially based on a Dutch text by Arjan Dasselaar (2004) to describe Internet search tools. It also reuses Wikipedia's description of its own services as a description of a social content intermediary.
- The idea of making this book initially resulted in criticism from my colleagues, which was useful for sharpening the idea and intentions behind it. I especially thank Lucas Meertens for his constructive contributions.
- I very much appreciate the encouraging talks with Adri Pater, who also has been so kind to critically read a less well-written draft and provided many good ideas for Chapter 5.

xviii *Acknowledgments*

- This book has been tested during an introductory course for Public Administration and Business Administration students at the University of Twente in 2008. I thank all the students who participated in this course for their constructive criticism and their patience with a still immature textbook. I also want to thank my student assistants Bart van Manen, Jef Martens, Hans Brilman and Martyn van de Wal, who have given substantial and useful comments to improve this book.
- The book has also been used at the University of Muenster as part of a course on Information Management in spring 2009. I appreciate the many debates with students in Muenster, and like to thank Stefan Klein for giving me this great opportunity.

Thank you all. I feel comfortable in accepting the full responsibility for this text.

Fons Wijnhoven
Enschede, The Netherlands

1 Introduction

Motivation and core idea

Information is any *representation* of our physical or imaginary world which people need to understand the world for problem solving and decision making. It is true that also animals, plants, and even physical systems use information, but we leave these types of information to the respective disciplines of biology, medicine, physics, or other related disciplines (for an interesting broader discussion of the concept of information see, for example, Stamper, 1973). Focal in our view is the human being as an intelligent being with high cognitive capabilities (like analysis, theorizing, and debating). In the context of the human use of representations a number of conceptual complications exist regarding my statement about information and representation. For example, two difficulties are:

1   What is the relation between a representation and its informative content?
2   How can information contribute to the capabilities of people to improve their situation?

The concept of *information* is often equated with data, and even more specifically to electronic data stored in databases or distributed via a data communication facility. The fact that much of the data we can get out of databases or via the Internet is actually incorrect, and even misinformation, points us to the need to be more careful here. Three reasons for being cautious are discussed below.

First of all, electronic media are not the only carriers of data as we may also have data in the form of *signs* (like written data, paintings, and pictures) and speech (also named *verbal* data) but indeed electronic media have an unprecedented level of efficiency. The reason for this efficiency is the extremely high commonality of electronic data and electronic data processing equipment, which are able to codify all data as binary units, i.e. + or − on magnetic data storage devices and 1 or 0 in code processing entities (Jonscher, 1994). The ASCII table is an example of such a coding of the alphabet which is shared by nearly all computers. There is no industry which has this level of commonality, and consequently the costs of data processing have been immensely reduced in the last decades, resulting in firms which have a global presence and a potential customer base of several 100 millions. At the same time, data processing serves the needs of nearly all individuals and organizations. Information is a key resource for strategic and operational processes in organizations, and data-carrying and processing machines are able to hugely reduce information collection, storage, manipulation, and distribution costs. In fact, the marginal reproduction and distribution costs of information-carrying data are nearly zero (Shapiro and Varian, 1999). The real costs, though, are the creation of the first copy. Information processing also has developed as a huge business in modern times. For instance, the IT consulting industry is estimated to be worth around 300 billion US dollars in 2007,[1] software firm Microsoft's shares were worth 325 billion dollars,[2] and IT service provider CISCO had a stock value of almost 152 billion US dollars on April 28, 2008.[3]

Second, the concept of "data" is quite complex and at least four types can be identified (Floridi, 2005):

1   *Primary data* are the principal data stored in a database and which an information system can deliver to a user.
2   *Metadata* enable a database management system to fulfill its tasks by describing essential properties of the primary data, like its origin, format, availability, and copyrights.
3   *Operational data* are data regarding the usage of the primary data, which may help the owners of information services, like online newspapers, to improve and customize their data to user needs or making the data more easily accessible.
4   *Derivative data* are data that can be created on basis of the first three types. For instance, stock exchange systems can deliver statistical data and statistical analysis. The primary data of a stock exchange consists of data on the price of stocks of different companies and the people who have offered and bought them on a certain day. The metadata of a stock exchange database may consist of availability rights of these data. For example, traders may have online access to the data and access to a system to offer and buy stocks. The general public may only have the right to see that database after a certain time has passed and may have access to the general statistics of a day. The managers of the stock exchange system need information on its performance to guarantee the quality of access for its subscribers and potentially interfere when certain transaction volumes seem to become alarming. Stock exchange analysts may be interested in derivative data products that analyze the performance of their buying and sales policies, so that they advise on certain tactics in selling and buying of stocks.

Third, the actual *contribution* of data to understanding of the real world is complex. We can, for instance, easily calculate the number of data available on our hard disk by seeing how many kilo-, mega-, or gigabytes are occupied by our documents, but this does not say much about our understanding of the world. Sometimes even less is better. Our example above of the stock exchange also pointed to the need of doing something with data to be able to make wise decisions by creating derivative data. So the key point with information management is not just data management, because *data are carriers and not the informing content itself*. But what is informative content? Floridi (2005 and 2007) mentions at least two criteria for data to be informative, and we can add a third one to the list below:

1   The data must be *meaningful*, i.e. people should be able to understand the message in the language they use. This seems to be an obvious criterion but many data in information systems may be incorrectly understood. Examples here are personnel information systems, where sometimes the number of people contracted are taken as the number of employees. But many contracted people may not have an employee contract and are hired, for example, via their consulting firm to help in a project. This problem of matching the meanings of users and information systems is named information *semantics* and is a key prerequisite for any successful information system.
2   The data must be *true*. Indeed, incorrect data do not help understanding the world, and in fact complicates the realization of understandings. Sometimes incorrect information is the result of unintentional behavior (named misinformation), but sometimes information is also intentionally incorrect to confuse the competition (named disinformation).
3   The data must be *relevant* for decision making and problem solving, which is also named the *pragmatic* function of information (Guetzkow, 1965). Having much meaningful and true information does not always mean that this information is relevant for the specific needs and context of its owner. In fact, sometimes too much meaningful and true information may result in information overload, which implies that the receiver of this information is not able to see the wood for the trees (Landau, 1969).

These considerations of the relation between data and information have been discussed in the philosophy of knowledge (epistemology) intensively, because they have been fundamental to management and administration since mankind began, as is manifest from, for example, the role of writing in the ancient Chinese administration and the role of documentation in pyramid building in ancient Egypt (George, 1972). Five fundamental paradigms of the nature of human information have developed and been codified by epistemological (knowledge theory) traditions. These paradigms are:

1   *Empiricism* (based on the philosophy of Locke), which is a theory of knowledge emphasizing the role of experience, especially sensory perception, in the formation of ideas, while discounting the notion of innate ideas.

2   *Rationalism* (Leibniz), which is any view appealing to reason as a source of knowledge or justification. In more technical terms it is a method or theory in which the criterion of truth is not sensory but intellectual and deductive.

3   *Kantianism.* Kant's main issue is the need of different perspectives that have to be taken to realize a complete picture of a phenomenon. This requires ways of integrating and consolidating sometimes conflicting perspectives.

4   *Hegelian dialectics.* In classical philosophy, dialectic logic is an exchange of propositions (theses) and counter-propositions (antitheses) resulting in a synthesis of the opposing assertions, or at least a qualitative transformation in the direction of the dialogue. In fact, dialectic logic had been introduced by Kant before as a way of consolidating different perspectives. Theses and antitheses, though, are carried by different people, who may have antagonistic interests, which is a key issue in Hegelian epistemology (Mason and Mitroff, 1973: 481). Consequently, informing becomes part of the political and competitive scene.

5   *Singerian pragmatism*, which is an epistemology and ethical theory stating that the value of knowledge should be expressed in terms of how the knowledge improves the human condition and, although people have to strive for truth, they will never reach the ultimate truth and human progress itself is even more important than truth itself.

These philosophies have not only inspired philosophers but are at the core of modern thinking about information and the use of computers and the Internet to support information management. This book provides the reader with key lessons of these philosophies and their implications for modern ways of information management. Information management is here understood as any *purposeful* individual and/or organizational activity by which information is handled. This statement is a bit vague and abstract, but the reader will recognize the usefulness of these philosophies for making information management a job of everyday life, by learning to model reality in the perspectives of these philosophies and making concrete use of computers to help them make sense of data and reality.

We may summarize the key statements of these philosophers about information as follows. According to Locke, information is a fact; according to Leibniz, real information is incorporated in the models by which we understand the reality. Following Kant there are many competing ways of looking at reality, sometimes resulting in useful complementary insights, and Hegel would probably regard information as a means for people with different views of reality to support their interests. The Lockean and Leibnizian models emphasize the need for objective information, whereas the Kantian view emphasizes the subjectivity of information. The Hegelian view emphasizes the action dimension of information, and the Singerian view emphasizes progress. These statements have substantial consequences for organizational processes (like decision making), knowledge creation, and the type of information systems which may be supportive to information management in organizations. See Table 1.1 for a summary of these views.

Note that, in the context of this book, we aim at a more detailed and fundamental understanding of the *concept of information* than is mostly common in the information systems field. In the information systems field, information is often equaled with knowledge derived from data, processed data, or data presented in a meaningful context (e.g. Kroenke, 2008: 24). This would imply that knowledge is "something" produced from data, but, for example, the Leibnizian approach would state that knowledge can be derived directly from good human thinking, so (nearly) no data processing is needed. Also, data can have a value by themselves, as stated by Locke, and sometimes data are intentionally used (i.e. they have a pragmatic purpose) for influencing the world (Hegel). This book, therefore, prefers more fundamental insights created by philosophical traditions. A more intuitive approach to the notion of information would not cover the potential information has as a social phenomenon for human problem solving and organizations.

Also note that I use the concept of *information system* in a more restricted sense than is common by many information scientists. It is frequently stated that an information system is "a group of components that interact to produce information" (Kroenke, 2008: 6). While identifying these components, they mention at least five: hardware, software, data, procedures, and people. I find this definition problematic, because it nearly includes everything of what we would call an organization, and thus has insufficient focus. I therefore restrict the notion of information systems to software and databases used for informing. Hardware is part of the information management infrastructure, and people and procedures are important parts of the strategic and organizational application domain (also see Chapter 6). This division of aspects related to informing and information systems is absolutely important for the division of labor and expertise in these fields. One cannot expect computer scientists to be able to solve problems in the organizational domain, although they may contribute from their expertise. The same applies for human relations experts and computer science problems.

Figure 1.1 summarizes this introductory discussion of data, information, and knowledge.

Approach and objectives

This book aims to provide a full understanding of information management. With full understanding we follow David Kolb's statements that knowledge can have two basic dimensions (abstract versus concrete, and reflection

Table 1.1 Implications of epistemological approaches for decision making, knowledge creation, and relevant information systems

	Locke	Leibniz	Kant	Hegel	Singer
Definition of information?	Data, facts, and figures	Knowledge, a model	Perspectives and integrated (nomological) theory	A thesis from some perspective and stakeholder and synthesis	Useful insight
Knowledge creation process	Induction; Observation; Classification; Communication	Deduction; Mathematical analysis; Formal logic	Multiple models; Integrated models	Construct thesis and antithesis; Dialectic logic; Synthesis	Learning from the interaction of theory and practice
Information systems	Databases and repositories	Decision support and expert systems	Integrated data and knowledge systems: knowledge-based systems	Internet and its tools for understanding	Documentations of experiences and insights; tools for collaborating in problem solving

Partially based on Courtney (2001).

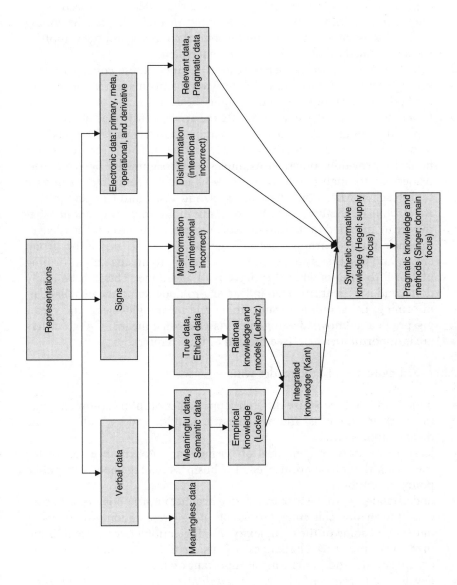

Figure 1.1 From representation to knowledge.

versus experimentation), and that learning is a process of progressive cycles between these (Kolb, 1984). Following this, we aim for:

1   *Abstract understanding*: this implies that some basic terminology is explained. This will be done by explaining the different perspectives on the notion of information and informing in each chapter, beginning with a discussion of the main philosophical concepts and their implications for a method of information management.
2   *Experimentation*: we challenge readers to apply these concepts in the management of information by providing information management methods and techniques and describing these.
3   *Concrete experience*: we demonstrate the applicability of abstract philosophical notions and related information management methods and techniques to solving concrete everyday problems. This is realized in this book by providing practical examples and assignments by which the reader has to analyze concrete problems using existing mass-software tools (such as Microsoft's Access, Excel, and Visio, and Google tools).
4   *Reflection*: we challenge readers to think in a critical way about what they read and tried in the assignment. We invite them to find challenges for their future learning career. A good way to do this is by group effort, and it is therefore advisable for readers to arrange an informing platform to discuss what they have read and done. This can be easily done, and is a great first step in learning to understand the challenge of informing, i.e. avoiding misinforming and meaninglessness, and creating pragmatic knowledge together via electronic means. Google offers great opportunities here (see the end of this chapter).

After reading this book, the reader will:

• understand and recognize different approaches of information management, their strengths and weaknesses, and the added value of the distinct approaches;
• learn to create simple models of business and governance reality for specifying the information needs for business management and public policy execution;
• understand key problems of translating abstract information needs to concrete information collecting, processing, and representation procedures;
• understand some of the complexity of information governance in organizations and the challenges of using information systems in organizations; and, maybe most important of all;
• develop *reflective and analytic capabilities to reason about information, informing, information management, and the use of information technologies*. These capabilities will be of value throughout your career and will enable you to critically diagnose and reap the opportunities of any new transient information technology in the future. As such I aim

at discussing information management as an *inherent human capability* instead of its supportive technologies.

These lessons, insights, and skills are key for any student at the undergraduate level of Business Administration, Public Administration, Social Sciences, and Economics. But this book may serve any person with an interest in the fundamentals of information and informing.

What is informing? A pragmatist approach and structure of this book

The question "What is informing?" is approached here from a pragmatist perspective, i.e. this book only handles the epistemological challenges as far as they are practical for the field of informing. Informing in such a context is a *purposeful* set of *activities* and *means* for collecting and making reusable representations for understanding the world. These "means" may include computers and data communication systems, but for successful informing they also include several organizational components. For making effective use of these "means," people need methodologies, which prescribe certain sets of activities to accomplish the goals of the user.

Informing is a process happening in a context. In this book the main context we consider is an organization. An organization may be viewed from a harmony or conflict perspective (Burrell and Morgan, 1979) or from a systems rational (one goal and a coherent system) or segmented institutional (i.e. multiple goals and ambitions aimed at by different stakeholders and parties) perspective (Kling, 1980). These views differ on what is believed to be an essential (i.e. ontological) characteristic of an organization, and define key aspects of the context of informing. The combined epistemological and ontological paradigms result in four views on informing. This book follows a pragmatic perspective on these views, assuming that each view has some relevance for solving real information management problems (Churchman, 1971; Mason and Mitroff, 1973). Table 1.2 identifies four approaches of informing, based on the four approaches of Table 1.1 and the two key ontological understandings of the organizational context of information systems.

These approaches can be integrated in a pragmatic way. Such a *pragmatic approach* starts with indicators for the world's problems and challenges for people and next selects potential knowledge (i.e. theories, methods, and technologies) that may be useful to find the most relevant insights to solve the problems. To actually solve the problem, the existing knowledge base will nearly never provide a direct solution, and a design project is needed to find solutions by an interaction of knowledge and concrete problem and problem-context information. The solution thus first will have to be designed, next will have to be tested, and on the basis of the test results can be implemented in the organizational context and be a potential

Table 1.2 Four views on informing integrated with ontological understandings of their organizational context

Ontology	Epistemology	
	Objectivism	Subjectivism
Systems rationalism	Lockean informing: Databases as answer providers	Leibnizian informing: Models of reality as the fence to look at the world.
Segmented institutionalism	Kantian informing: Different but complementary views of the world	Hegelian informing: Different views based on people's stakes in reality and ways of finding syntheses via dialectic logic

source for updating the knowledge base in the related academic field. The problems and challenges this book focuses on are within the context of an organization, consisting of people, organizational structures, and their technologies for handling its challenges. The knowledge people have available for creating understanding of their world consists of theories based on the four views on information, related methods for handling information of relevance, and tools for increasing the efficiency in information handling. This pragmatic scientific approach is summarized by Hevner *et al.* (2004) under the name "design science." See Figure 1.2.

This book will first discuss the four main philosophical approaches to information management and its methods and techniques in Chapters 2–5, before we start discussing informing in the more complex organizational context. Therefore, the next four chapters will discuss the Lockean, Leibnizian, Kantian, and Hegelian philosophies and their consequences for methods and tools of informing. These discussions will be illustrated by examples in each chapter. Next, we further discuss the organizational context in which informing takes place in Chapter 6. It is true that informing also happens in everyday life outside the context of organizations, but organizations are able to collect and organize substantially large resources so that informing may happen at a much more refined and advanced level as we would be able to do individually. (That is indeed a key ambition of organizations; Barnard, 1938.) And finally we will discuss in Chapter 7 the design science approach to informing and information management, as continuous processes of problem solving and knowledge creation in design and justification projects.

As the author is not a philosopher but an information scientist who is happy to be able to *use* substantial philosophical research results for the improvement of his discipline, you can acknowledge that this book is not a study about philosophy. Many others have done a part of this already. Some of the major authors here are Mason and Mitroff (1973), who based their insights on the work of C. W. Churchman (1971). *The Stanford Encyclopedia*

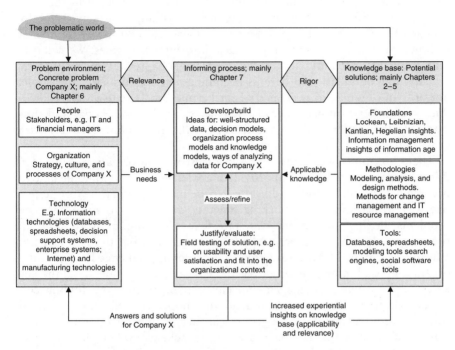

Figure 1.2 A model of the pragmatic perspective on informing.

Source: Based on Hevner *et al.* (2004).

of Philosophy is used as a resource to gain insights on each of these philosophers and these texts are commented on from a more up-to-date perspective (especially the innovative tools supplied by Microsoft and Google). The work of Churchman (and Mason and Mitroff) has obvious limitations, as it does not discuss well the organizational consequences of these philosophies, which is most fundamental for business and public administration students. Consequently, an article of Courtney (2001) is used to discuss the organizational consequences. The work of many other information scientists is used to describe a match between philosophical notions of information and the modern tools to informing. A full list of the references is given at the end of the book, but each chapter also mentions literature for further reading.

Reflective practice by social software

The stories about Locke, Leibniz, Kant, Hegel, and Singer demonstrate that informing is a very old discipline. This has the advantage that I can safely base my fundamental insights on these ideas, as they have been appealing to mankind in the past and probably still will inspire people in the next ages to come. But, we cannot easily say that informing in our days is totally similar to informing in the past few ages. This is so because of the rise of information technologies to support us in informing processes. We will present some key technologies in the next few chapters. One technology already may be mentioned here as becoming a set of tools for all people, not only in organizations. This tool set I name "social software." I introduce social software here, because it is a key tool for learning, and thus may help the reader to discuss and work with this book collectively with other readers.

There are many ways how one can digest new information, but when this information is expected to provide knowledge, it also should be able to become new work practice. Additionally, one may state that the most effective way of learning is by working together on a topic to solve complex problems. In this context one can state that informing, as being a group process, is not only an academically interesting topic, but the very heart of effective learning. Having said this, the reader is challenged to join and organize mutual informing processes to help each other understand the key issues of information management. This can be realized by finding colleagues or friends who want to read this book as well and use social software tools to facilitate the group learning. A good overview of social software tools gives Wikipedia and www.lifehacker.com. Google offers several social software tools, like opportunities for creating discussion groups on specific topics and creating blogs and shared agenda tools to plan the process of reading and performing reflective tasks. To help the reader start up with social software, the following activities may be considered:

- Set up a group blog and create your group's discussion forum and agenda in Google.
- Review Google Docs for opportunities for co-writing. This can enable the group to share notes and thoughts and bundle them in a shared document.
- Create a work and study plan (i.e. internal delivery and discussion schedules in detail, including proposed tools to be used) in Google Agenda shared by the group.
- Make a discussion forum in Google Groups to discuss issues.
- Plan the deliverables made in Google Docs in the group agenda.

Further reading

Elementary further reading

Kroenke, D. M. (2008) *Experiencing Management Information Systems.* Upper Saddle River, NJ: Pearson Prentice Hall, pp. 2–35.

On social software

Kroenke, D. M. (2008) *Experiencing Management Information Systems.* Upper Saddle River, NJ: Pearson Prentice Hall, pp. 317–327.

On epistemologies

Churchman, C. W. (1971) *The Design of Inquiring Systems: Basic Concepts of Systems and Organization.* New York: Basic Books.

On the application of Churchman's insight into information management and organization

Courtney, J. (2001) "Decision making and knowledge management in inquiring organizations: Toward a new decision-making paradigm for DSS," *Decision Support Systems*, 31: 17–38.

Mason, R. and Mitroff, I. (1973) "A program for research on management information systems," *Management Science*, 19(5): 475–487.

On information and knowledge

Floridi, L. (2007) "Semantic conceptions of information," in E. N. Zalta (ed.) *The Stanford Encyclopedia of Philosophy* (Spring 2007 Edition), http://plato. stanford.edu/archives/spr2007/entries/information-semantic; accessed May, 2008.

Mingers, J. (2008) "Management knowledge and knowledge management: Realism and forms of truth," *Knowledge Research and Practice*, 6: 62–76.

Stamper, R. (1973) *Information in Business and Administrative Systems.* New York: Wiley.

On organization context and informing

Burrell, G. and Morgan, G. (1979) *Sociological Paradigms and Organizational Analysis: Elements of the Sociology of Corporate Life.* London: Heinemann.

George, C. (1972) *The History of Management Thought.* Englewood Cliffs, NJ: Prentice Hall.

Guetzkow, H. (1965) "Communication in organizations," in J. March (ed.) *Handbook of Organizations.* Chicago, IL: Rand McNally, pp. 534–573.

Kling, R. (1980) "Social aspects of computing: Theoretical perspectives in recent empirical research," *Computing Surveys*, 12: 61–110.

2 The Lockean view and databases

Introduction to the philosophy of John Locke

John Locke[1]

John Locke is considered the first of the British Empiricists, but is equally important to social contract theory. His ideas had enormous influence on the development of epistemology and political philosophy, and he is widely regarded as one of the most influential Enlightenment thinkers and contributors to liberal theory. His writings influenced Voltaire and Rousseau, many Scottish Enlightenment thinkers, as well as the American revolutionaries. He postulated in his first book on *An Essay Concerning Human Understanding* that there are no innate ideas that form our understanding of the world. In Book II he states that the mind is a "blank slate" or "tabula rasa;" that is, contrary to Cartesian or Christian philosophy, Locke maintained that people are born without innate ideas. In Book III he states that language is a key element in forming and codifying understandings, and that we need to share common meanings to make knowledge sharing feasible. Locke recognizes that ordinary people are the chief makers of language and that scientists have the task of checking if the connections made between properties in reality made in this language are actually true (or not). In Book IV Locke states that man should try to use reason, i.e. a combination of observation, experience, and rationality in finding truth. But, man has limitations in reasoning, simply because many issues are so complex that people lack sufficient experiences, observations, and valid theories, for the time being, and in such cases it is reasonable to believe, i.e. reason by faith through a communication with God and traditional revelation. So revelation comes in where reason cannot reach. Locke also identifies so-called "enthusiasts," i.e. "those who would abandon reason and claim to know on the basis of faith alone" (Uzgalis, 2007, p. 25). Locke regrets this attitude, which explains why he was not always very popular among representatives of the church, but contributed substantially to new ideas in his time.

Empiricism is a theory of knowledge emphasizing the role of experience, especially sensory perception, in the formation of ideas. Indeed, the mind as tabula rasa needs some kind of mechanism for data collection and acquisition. It is a fundamental requirement of empirical science methods that all hypotheses and theories must be tested against observations of the natural world, rather than resting solely on a priori reasoning, intuition, or revelation. The term "empiricism" has a dual etymology. It comes from the Greek word εμπειρισμὸζ, the Latin translation of which is *experientia*, from which we derive the word "experience." It also derives from a more specific classical Greek and Roman usage of *empiric*, referring to a physician whose skill derives from practical experience as opposed to instruction in theory and dogmas.

Empiricism does not hold that we have empirical knowledge automatically. Rather, according to the empiricist view, for any knowledge to be properly inferred or deduced, it is to be gained ultimately from one's sense-based experience, which requires an experience or data collection mechanism and ways of labeling, classifying, and describing these experiences. To let these experiences converge to knowledge (explanations, predictions, or methodologies) they will have to be analyzed and the insights must be shared by the community of experts. Furthermore, Locke, for his part, held that some knowledge could be arrived at through intuition (e.g. knowledge of God's existence) and reasoning (e.g. mathematics) alone, and thus does not need experiential evidence, but his main contribution is his emphasis on the value of experience and data. Some other philosophers commonly associated with empiricism include Francis Bacon, Thomas Hobbes, George Berkeley, David Hume, and John Stuart Mill. Figure 2.1 gives a model of the interactions between the individual and its problematic world during the process of empirical knowledge creation.

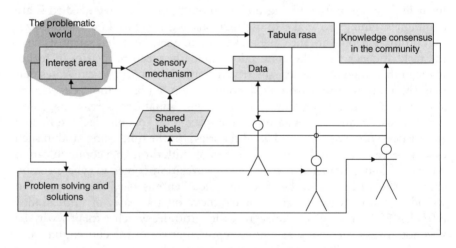

Figure 2.1 Interaction between person and problematic world in the process of data collection and knowledge creation by the Lockean community.

Consequences for information management

John Locke seems to have been a philosopher with a wide area of interests. For this book, though, we will focus on his work on epistemology, i.e. the philosophy of knowing and empiricism in particular. According to empiricism, the key to any understanding of the world is our way of collecting information via our senses, and next analyzing it. Our senses thus are data collection mechanisms, and the data we collect are more or less directly understandable and can be shared with other people to develop a collective understanding. However, data collection and knowledge creation cannot be automated and require substantial working of the mind. The mind, for instance, will have to develop interests in specific areas (trying to collect all data about everything is obviously impossible) related to specific challenges and goals of the person. These interests and goals thus delimit the boundaries of the *universe of discourse*, which in its turn specifies the data needed and the mechanisms by which these data can be efficiently and effectively acquired (the so-called sensory mechanism). These data need interpretation and analysis to create relevant information for decision making and problem solving, but an important bias is actually already created by the sensory mechanism itself. Interesting examples here are the many types of registered contracts which are comparable to a marriage in the Netherlands, whereas many other societies only recognize one type of marriage. Another example is the many words Inuit people are supposed to use for "snow." Some authors seem to suggest that there are even hundreds of these words. This, interestingly enough, is not the result of a more detailed distinction in Inuit languages of the phenomenon of snow itself, but the consequence of the large diversity of Inuit languages and the *syntactic* (i.e. coding and grammar rules) structure of their languages (Martin, 1986). Consequently, making a universe of discourse description is not only a matter of choosing a proper scope of phenomena to incorporate (and to exclude what is regarded as irrelevant), but also to choose and agree on the coding and words for representing these phenomena.

Summarizing these statements about John Locke's epistemology and empiricism, we can conclude that:

- data are created by sensory mechanisms, which we could name as the input side of an information repository or database, and have to be constructed by an active mind;
- these data are labeled representations of objects in reality;
- the labels have to fit with an agreed (consensual) set of labels so that data can be meaningfully shared among people through time (archives) and space (communication media), which enables us to make sense out of reality through discussion.

A key element missing in this description of empiricism is the context in which this philosophy developed popularity. Imagine Locke's seventeenth century. How many sensory mechanisms were available for business, public policy makers, and scientists to better understand their world for their problem-solving and decision-making jobs? What were these sensory mechanisms, how effective and efficient were these, and how complete were the resulting data as representations of the world? The answer is: not very complete. The data collection was a very labor-intensive process with manual data filing procedures consisting of handwritten reports and taking reports to specific archival locations, personal interviewing of people nearby (traveling was extremely costly), and archival search; consequently policy and decision making was based on a very limited data set. Much uncertainty had to be handled by trusting the wisdom (whatever the meaning of this word) of people who were given the power of decision making for others. What does the sensory mechanism look like in our current age? We have many databases, news-distributing media, and the Internet, which together are giving us a huge information overload (Landau, 1969). How can we make sense out of these data? At least two mechanisms are needed:

1   Data models which help to efficiently handle data (storage and retrieval), maintain consistency among different data sets, and ease the maintenance of data about information entities.
2   Reporting mechanisms, which enable us to quickly produce relevant reports out of the many data. This is by the specification of output-generating queries and reporting software.

Lockean epistemology and database development

A few key elements are central to the described Lockean model for information management, because they consist of four steps of creating understanding of the world by managing information:

1   The development of focused human interest in certain aspects or areas of the world, which results in a universe of discourse, i.e. the area which is under consideration, and thus excludes other areas.
2   The creation of a *model* of the universe of discourse. A model is a simplified representation of a piece of reality consisting of entities and relations; in the case of information management these entities are objects about which data are collected, and these entities may have certain logical relations, which when well understood ease the maintenance of consistency of data and the creation of information outputs from the data.
3   The entity-relationship models can be used to design the most efficient structure of a database.
4   The current age enables us to use database software to efficiently manage the data collected, maintain the data, and create relevant information from these data for problem solving and decision making.

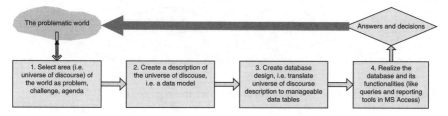

Figure 2.2 A process model of the Lockean epistemology and the role of databases.

Figure 2.2 gives a four-step process model of this epistemology, starting from problem recognition and finishing with answers and decisions, with the role of databases included. Each of these four steps is further described below.

Select universe of discourse

Although this step may be technically the easiest, it is often the most difficult, and the so-called *Lockean community* is not that easy to create. The reasons are that different stakeholders may have different objectives and, therefore, want other data to be collected and reported. The interests also result in other problems, challenges, and goals, and therefore also other definitions of the scope or boundary of the universe of discourse may exist. In the context of project management, for instance, the project champion and sponsor may be much interested in a precise measurement of the spent resources (time, budget, and people) and concrete results according to the requirements. For project participants, though, it may be more important to have influence on who is participating in the project and how this may shape the work relations per task and the ultimate result. For department management, an insight into the concrete impact on the department's structure, technology, and ways of working are key, as well as the career opportunities of the people of the department involved. Consequently, different project management reports may be expected, and serving them all may be practically infeasible.

A possible result of such a scoping activity for project management may be to agree on the following project management *objects* to check:

1   Employees' involvement per department, and number of their hours per task, which may be key information for department managers.
2   Tasks, costs, time, and results with respect to achieved targets may be key information for project sponsors because they will have to pay.
3   An overview of departments involved and in what other projects the departments participate may be important information for the project champion.

The resulting objects of the universe of discourse are presented in Figure 2.3.

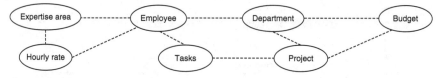

Figure 2.3 A universe of discourse for project management.

In everyday life, the creation of a universe of discourse is not easy. For instance, have you ever tried to exchange (business) contact information with others? If not, try it, and you will quickly find out that each of your friends will probably have a different way of registering their contacts, because everyone will use different labels (e.g. "telephone" instead of "phone") and some use more attributes than others (e.g. have included full address with area codes, while some might not have the address at all, or addresses without area codes). This difference makes the automatic merging of personal databases nearly impossible.

Universe of discourse description and entity relation models

A universe of discourse can be further described by the entities, their attributes, and their relationships.

An *entity* is an element from the universe of discourse that someone wants to track, like employee participation in projects, the number of projects and their costs and results, and the involvement of departments in projects. Consequently, entities, which as a convention are always singular, may be "Department," "Project," and "Employee." Entities have *attributes* that describe characteristics of the entity. For department, these may be the department name, and department address. For projects the attributes may be project name project number, project deadline, project tasks, and project task number. Employees have a name, a personnel number, a function, an hourly rate, address, and phone number. Entities must have an *identifier*, which is an attribute or group of attributes whose value is associated with *one and only one* entity instance. For example, employees mostly cannot be uniquely identified by their name only, and thus a unique personnel number is needed in addition. For administrative efficiency, departments, projects, and budgets mostly have unique numbers as well.

Entities have *relationships* with each other. An employee, for instance, has a relationship with a department (department members) and one or more projects (project participation). Projects have several participants (i.e. employees). Sponsors may have several projects. The relations between the entities can be 1:1, 1:N, M:1, or M:N. In the case of the relation between departments and employees, one department may have several employees; this relation will be 1:N when the organization requires an employee to be a member of only one department. The relation between department and project may be M:N, when several departments participate in a project, and when departments can participate in several projects. These relations are for ease of communication and documentation often represented by so-called crow's feet (see, for example, Kroenke, 2008: 363). The crow's foot notation shows the maximum cardinality in a relationship. For instance, the 1:N relation between department and organization member gives a constraint of 1 to the number of departments an employee can be a member of. A *minimum cardinality* also can be given, stating that the entity department cannot be empty. In some cases a database may allow for the project entity to be empty (simply, when there are no projects undertaken at a certain moment), or one may allow certain attributes to be optional, e.g. an employee has a cell phone. The first is expressed by a zero instead of a crow or line connection with the entity. An alternative method for entity-relationship modeling is named object role modeling (ORM). MS-visio uses ovals with closed lines to represent ORM entities, and it uses ovals with dashed lines to represent ORM attributes. Relations between entities and between entities and attributes are represented by roles, which are comparable to the columns of a table. Identifiers are presented by arrows over a role, which denote the uniqueness constraint for the attribute, i.e. the role can be read as a table

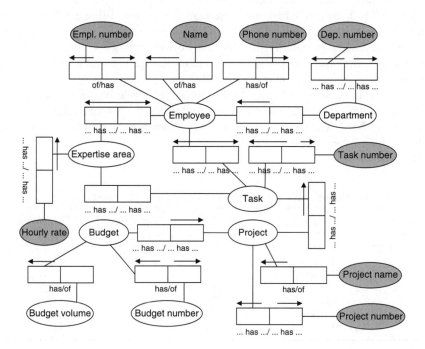

Figure 2.4 The project management ERD data model using MS-Visio ORM.

Note
White ovals denote entities; Shaded ovals denote attributes.

with only one occurrence of the entity under the arrow and multiple occurrences of the attribute in the role without an arrow. See Figure 2.4 for a possible ORM/ERD (Entity Relationship Diagram) of the project management universe of discourse of Figure 2.4.

The database design

The third step in the Lockean epistemology for information management is to put the entity relationship model into a design of an efficient repository of information. Such a repository may in a simple case consist of a table named according to the entity and a set of columns indicating the attributes of the entity. In practice, though, the situation may be more complicated, as we may want to manage relations among data of different entities and to register quite a few attributes of an entity. The problem in such a situation is that, when the attributes and the data are going to change, a quite common thing in real life, the large size of the data may result in inconsistencies in the database. The inconsistency is what database experts name the *data integrity problem*.

In the example, we may have changes related to the entities "department" and "employee." For instance, departments may merge. Tables 2.1 and 2.2 show what happens when we create an Employee Table with employee number, employee name, phone number, department number, and department name when two departments (Finance and Strategic Consulting) decide to merge. After the merger, we will have to change the name of the department for each employee entry separately.

Indeed, in each of the rows of the Employee Table one has to check if a change of department name is needed, and it is quite essential that no errors are made here. This is a tedious and error-prone job, which can be more easily done by separating employee and department data.

Table 2.1 Employee Table before merger of Departments 1 and 2

Employee number	Employee name	Phone number	Department number	Department name
1	Johnson	224455	1	Finance
2	Williams	337799	2	Strategy
3	Bergman	234567	3	IT
4	Gade	135790	1	Finance
5	Fialkowski	554433	2	Strategy
6	Johnson	779922	3	IT

Note
The change will have to be implemented as often as Departments 1 and 2 have employees (in the example four times); whereas a single Department Table only would need two changes (department name and number).

Table 2.2 Normalized Employee Table after merger

Employee number (Primary key)	Employee name	Phone number	Department number (Foreign key)
1	Johnson	224455	1
2	Williams	337799	1
3	Bergman	234567	2
4	Gade	135790	1
5	Fialkowski	554433	1
6	Johnson	779922	2

Department number (Primary key)	Department name
1	Finance and strategy
2	IT

Note
The department number is a foreign key, and thus will be automatically updated when changes happen in the Department Table. When an employee switches between departments, this only has to be updated for the individual employee number.

One may say that department mergers are not so common, and therefore the problem will be easily manageable without databases. Agreed, but a lot of other data may change frequently. For instance, cell phone numbers may change every few years and people may switch between departments and teams. Also, in commercial settings, data changes frequently. For instance, in a nationally operating grocery chain, numbers of products in stock change each operating day at all different stocks, and products are replaced frequently. These database changes have a huge impact on the operational activities of such a firm. Procurement managers, logistics and distribution service providers, financial managers, warehouse managers, and sales managers all need the same *consistent* data each day. The cause of data integrity problems is the existence of duplicated or *redundant* data. So the solution is to minimize redundancy through splitting tables into themes which probably will not need redundant data. This effort is also named *database normalization*. The links between the two new tables is realized by placing the "primary key" for the Department Table in a column of the Employee Table (which has Employee Number as the primary key, i.e. unique identifier of an entry).

The normalization of Table 2.1 is given in Table 2.2.

So how can we transfer a data model to an efficient database design?

1 *Step 1* here is to create tables for each entity, with an entity identifier and columns per attribute.

2   *Step 2* is the normalization of the resulting tables.
3   *Step 3* is the realization of the relations between the entities as defined in the ERD. This can be done by placing identifiers of the tables that have to be connected with the focal entity as a column attribute. To avoid redundancy in the tables, in a 1:N relation we place the identifier of the entity that will not be repeated in the table of the entity that will be repeated (and not the other way round, as that would imply a M:1 relation). Identifiers that form the primary keys (unique identifiers of entities) are mostly represented by the PK acronym, and the PK of other tables are presented as foreign keys (FK) to denote relations.
4   *Step 4* is the implementation of N:M relations, which implies a separate table with repetitions in the combined columns.
5   *Step 5.* Relations between tables are often presented by arrows between tables that share keys. The arrows point in the direction of the table with the primary key. See Figure 2.5.

Figure 2.5 gives a translation of Figure 2.4, mentioned in the previous subsection, in which for each entity separate tables have been created, and foreign keys are assigned depending on the roles. One can use MS-Visio to design the database structure. MS-Visio also enables you to check the consistency and normalization of your database design.

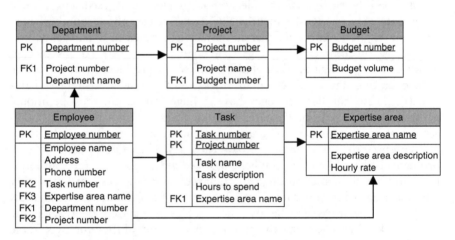

Figure 2.5 A database design of the project management ERD of Figure 2.4.

Working with database software: MS-Access

There are many interesting and very professional database software systems, which enable companies to manage thousands of entities, with an even larger number of attributes, such that integrity is realized to a certain extent, while thousands of users access and modify data and attributes each day. This is advanced work, which is not discussed here (for further details see Kroenke, 2008, pp. 99–110, and Hoffer *et al.*, 2002), but it is useful to show some of the practical issues by going to MS-Access. MS-Access is a widely used database system for personal use and some small business environments, but working with it gives a good sense of what information management in the Lockean sense nowadays involves.

Table 2.3 Converting the database design to an MS-Access database

Lockean system element	MS-Access tool	For the project management case
Specify boundary of universe of discourse by mentioning entities	Open MS-Access, create a new database with a name (boundary). Create tables for each entity. Give data types for each identifier and attribute. Remark: MS-Access names an "attribute" a "field," and an "identifier" is a field with a "primary key."	Create the project management database and tables with data types per attribute and identifier.
Create relationships	Open the Relationship window of Access and create relationship. MS-Access enables this by dragging identifiers of other tables into and on top of other tables. The dragged identifiers become foreign keys in the other tables.	Implement the foreign keys in the tables.
Create the sensory mechanism (data acquisition facility)	Create a data entry form by opening Tables using the Form Wizard. Next fill the forms with data.	Create forms to insert employee, department, and project data.
Retrieve relevant collected data	Create queries using the query design tool of MS-Access.	Create queries to generate data concerning actual costs (i.e. hourly rates, hours per task, and total) and budget per project.
Create relevant decisional information	Use the Report Wizard to create reports.	Make a nice layout for a report.

Working with MS-Access enables the efficient handling of the key elements of the Lockean system as summarized in Table 2.3. Kroenke (2008) and the MS-Access manual give useful and easy examples and tutorials of working with MS-Access. Basically, one can get control over MS-Access in around four hours. An easy way of working with MS-Access is to use its *wizards*.

The wizards enable the creation of tables, queries, forms, and reports. A simple example of creating a query is to combine the two parts of the Normalized Employee Table (Table 2.2) in a single view such as Table 2.1. If the database relations have been entered according to Figure 2.5 and the data of Table 2.2 have been inserted, then creating the query is done in three steps:

1   Use "Create query by using wizard."
2   Add the right fields from the right tables (number and name from Department, and name, number, and phone number from Employee).
3   Click "Finish."

For most queries, it is advisable to look at the *design view*. This enables the simple creation of queries as well, but also offers the creation of advanced queries. The most complex queries can also be entered in the *SQL view*. Listing Table 2.1 provides the SQL view for combining the Normalized Employee Table (see Figure 2.6). This is the expert view, however, and requires knowledge of SQL, which is beyond the scope of this book.

Creating a report is almost as easy as creating a simple query. After starting the appropriate wizard, you have to select the fields from the tables you want to use, as Figure 2.7 shows.

The next page of the wizard allows you to decide which field, if any, you want to use to group the data. After that, it is possible to select how the data is ordered, for example ascending by employee number. In most cases, it is also possible to select summary options. These allow you to aggregate data. Figure 2.8 shows a screenshot of these options.

Be aware that summary options should be considered carefully. For example, taking the average of the department numbers has no value as

```
Listing Table 2.1:
SELECT Department.[Department number]
AS [Department_Department number],
Department.[Department name], Employee.[Employee
number], Employee.[Employee name], Employee.[Phone
number], Employee.[Department number]
AS [Employee_Department number]
FROM Department INNER JOIN Employee ON
Department.[Department number] = Employee.[Department
number]
```

Figure 2.6 A listing of SQL statements.

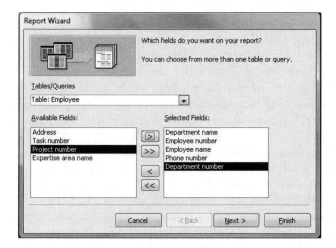

Figure 2.7 Example of the MS-Access report wizard.

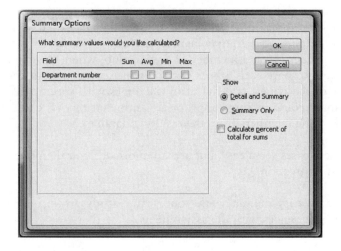

Figure 2.8 MS-Access summary options.

information. As the possibilities in the figure show, it is possible to do this. Also, keep in mind that the summary options are only applicable to numbers, not words. Further pages in the wizard allow you to determine the layout and design of the report. When the wizard is finished, the design view may be used to make adjustments.

Reflective practice

So what have you learned and how can you use it? Some of you may think at this moment that using databases is not relevant for practice, because mostly one may need only one table or a so-called flat file. Such readers may be right sometimes, but when the information needs become a bit more complex and when frequent data maintenance is needed, annoying and time-consuming inconsistencies can easily happen, and then databases may offer great opportunities. Try, for instance, the following:

- Manage your personal library, consisting of books which you frequently lend to your friends that you may want back. You will probably have to record data about the books and the persons who loaned them. How would the database look like? How can you easily make reports of what has been lent out? Maybe you even want to find out your friends' returning behavior. (Did you have to frequently request it back, and in what status did the books return?)
- Or, consider that you are in a group of former classmates who decide to organize a reunion of pupils and teachers for a whole day. The teachers also want to have a joint reunion for the last three years so that the school can sponsor 50 percent of it. What data do you have to register? What database design may be most useful?
- Or, consider being a member of a wine club, where the members have decided to share each other's data on wines, wine makers, their evaluations of the wines, and the fit of the wines with specific dishes. What database could be most appropriate and what reports could be generated by the members from the resulting database?

Indeed these cases seem easy, but are still more difficult than one may think of on first impression.

- Make an easy manual with your virtual study group on the basis of your experiences with the assignments.

Further reading

Elementary further reading

Kroenke, D. (2008) *Experiencing Management Information Systems*. Upper Saddle River, NJ: Pearson Prentice Hall, especially pp. 196–211, 359–394, and 493–505.

On databases

Hoffer, J. A., Prescott, M. B., and McFadden, F. R. (2002) *Modern Database Management*. Upper Saddle River, NJ: Prentice Hall.

On empiricist philosophy

Churchman, C. W. (1971) *The Design of Inquiring Systems: Basic Concepts of Systems and Organization*. New York: Basic Books.

Uzgalis, W. (2007) "John Locke," in E. N. Zalta (ed.) *The Stanford Encyclopedia of Philosophy* (Summer 2007 Edition), http://plato.stanford.edu/archives/sum2007/entries/locke; accessed May 2008.

On implications of empiricism to databases

Dietz, J. (2004) "Towards a LAP-based information paradigm," in M. Aakhus and M. Linds (eds.) *Proceedings of the 9th International Working Conference on the Language-Action Perspective on Communication Modeling*. New Brunswick, NJ: School of Communication, Information, and Library Studies, Rutgers, The State University of New Jersey, pp. 59–75.

Martin, L. (1986) "Eskimo words for snow: A case study in the genesis and decay of an anthropological example," *American Anthropologist*, 88(2): 418–423.

Nijssen, G. and Halpin, T. (1989) *Conceptual Schema and Relational Database Design: A Fact Oriented Approach*. New York: Prentice Hall.

On information overload

Landau, M. (1969) "Redundancy, rationality and the problem of duplication and overlap," *Public Administration Review*, 29(4): 346–358.

3   The Leibnizian view and decision models

Introduction to the philosophy of Leibniz

Leibniz[1]

Gottfried Wilhelm Leibniz (also Leibnitz) was educated in law and philosophy; serving as factotum to two major German noble houses, he played a major role in European politics and diplomacy (Wikipedia page on Leibniz, March 2008). He occupies an equally large place in both the history of philosophy and the history of mathematics. He discovered calculus independently of Newton, and his notation is the one in general use since then. He also discovered the binary system, the foundation of virtually all modern computer architectures. In philosophy, he is most remembered for optimism, i.e. his conclusion that our universe is, in a restricted sense, the best possible one God could have made. He was, along with René Descartes and Baruch Spinoza, one of the three great seventeenth-century rationalists. Leibniz also made major contributions to physics and technology, and anticipated notions that surfaced much later in biology, medicine, geology, probability theory, psychology, linguistics, and information science. He also wrote on politics, law, ethics, theology, history, and philology, and even occasional verse.

Rationalism is any view appealing to reason as a source of knowledge or justification (Churchman, 1971). It is a method or theory in which the criterion of truth is not sensory but intellectual and deductive. Different degrees of emphasis on this method or theory lead to a range of rationalist standpoints, from the moderate position that reason has precedence over other ways of acquiring knowledge, to the radical position that reason is the unique path to knowledge.

Within the Western philosophical tradition, rationalism begins with Plato, whose theory of the self-sufficiency of reason became the main idea of idealistic philosophy. Since the Enlightenment, rationalism is usually associated with the introduction of mathematical methods into philosophy, as in Descartes, Leibniz, and Spinoza. This is commonly called continental rationalism, because it was predominant in the continental schools of Europe, whereas in Britain empiricism dominated (see Chapter 2).

Rationalism is often contrasted with empiricism. Taken very broadly these views are not mutually exclusive, since a philosopher can be both rationalist and empiricist. Proponents of some varieties of rationalism argue that, starting with foundational basic principles, like the axioms of geometry, one could deductively derive the rest of all possible knowledge. Both Spinoza and Leibniz asserted that, *in principle*, all knowledge, including scientific knowledge, could be gained through the use of reason alone, though they both observed that this was not possible *in practice* and observations and data are important as well. The key point is, though, that the creation of knowledge is not based on the development of consensus in a group of experts, but that any person with the proper kind of logical and reasoning capabilities may be able to discover knowledge and models of reality on his or her own. It is not the community but rationality that determines truth.

A key insight of Leibniz is his "principle of sufficient reason," which states that nothing is without a reason and there is no effect without a cause (Look, 2008: 8). Although it may sometimes be difficult, people are able to discover these reasons and effects by their innate capability of the correct analysis of necessities and contingencies. In this, people are a specific kind of rational animal. Whereas, for example, dogs are able to observe *phenomena* and react automatically to their appearance (e.g. seeing a cat may result in the willingness to chase it), people are able to identify substances which compose reality, and more importantly still, people are able to identify the "soul," also named nomads of a substance. Knowing these nomads, people are able to understand the forces of these substances. The nomads and their striving to final causes are the result of the work of the perfect engineer or architect of the world, according to Leibniz God.

Leibniz states that people can strive for two kinds of truths: truth of *reasoning* and truth of *fact*. Truth of reasoning, i.e. necessary truth, can be discovered by the analysis of the notions, and "resolving it into simpler ideas and simpler truths until we reach the primitives" (Look, 2008: 24). The "principle of contradiction" is used to check if a truth of reasoning is indeed found, because contradiction is of course not acceptable. A truth of fact, i.e. a contingent truth, exists in the detection of certain correlations between phenomena, but does not provide causes and explanations. Look states (p. 26):

> According to Leibniz, while the empiricist position can explain the source of contingent truths, it cannot adequately explain the origin and character of necessary truths. For the senses could never arrive at the universality of any necessary truth; they can, at best, provide us with the means of making a relatively strong induction. Rather it is the understanding itself, Leibniz claims, which is the source of such truths and which guarantees their very necessity. While we are not aware of all our ideas at any time [. . .] certain ideas or truths are in our minds as dispositions or tendencies. This is what is meant by an innate idea or an innate truth.

Consequences for information management

It is good to know that, although rationalism is mainly appealing to a key capability of people (reasoning), even this philosophical approach sees value in experience, sensing, and data. But, of course, what is data and experience without reasoning? Let us summarize the consequences of this Leibnizian view for information management:

1 In contrast to the empiricists, the rationalists regard correct reasoning about reality to be more important than large volumes of data. Large volumes of data may result in total chaos and confusion, whereas reasoning is the mechanism by which experiences can be evaluated and connected into true causal insights. Computers have capabilities of storing data, but they also have capabilities of emulating human reasoning, i.e. calculating and processing of logic operations, like "not," "and," and "or," as we know from using Internet search engines.

2 Computers cannot make useful logic operations without people who structure reality and provide the computer with correct representations of reality. For databases we need data models and data definitions as well as the insertion of data. Similarly, for getting computers to reason about reality, we have to give it a "picture" of this reality and related data. Such a "picture" we name a model, which identifies the key "substances" and their dispositions, i.e. nomads.

3 A model of reality must incorporate descriptions of a few phenomena whose dispositions may explain their behavior and how they impact on other parts (substances) of reality. Thus causality between independent and dependent variables must be well understood.

4 It is not necessary that the model is large, but it must have sufficient explanatory power. Because the world consists of huge numbers of substances, people, in their attempts to explain final causes, need to cut down on the number of substances and relations to focus on. Although indeed people have innate reasoning capabilities, people's reasoning capacity has certain limitations. This final statement is not directly derived from Leibniz, or Look's and Churchman's descriptions of Leibniz, but is an obvious issue, by which people will have difficulties achieving the same kind of understanding as "the world's architect."

5 The knowledge gained can be represented by models, which thus emulate the reasoning about the world. The model must have a "calculation" mechanism (which may include calculus or discrete mathematics, i.e. formal logic) to infer impacts of states of substances on the states of other substances. These states of substances can be measured and observed and, as such, they are independent variables. Note, though, that when talking about variables, we are applying an

empiricist language. In this empiricist (Lockean) language, we may identify independent and dependent variables, whose correlations should correspond with real causes identified in the rationalist language. The choice for these variables is based on reasoning, not sensation. The resulting empirical models thus may emulate expected and predicted behavior.

6   Most models can be implemented in computer software systems such as spreadsheets or decision support systems. In this, computers can emulate expected and predicted behavior by simulation of the real world (e.g. by "what-if analysis").

The differences of rationalism and empiricism are presented in Figure 3.1.

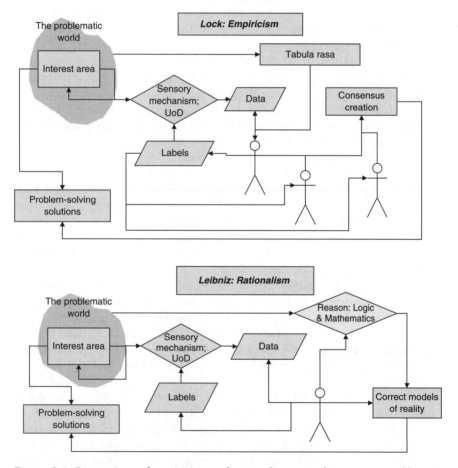

Figure 3.1 Comparison of empiricism and rationalism regarding person–problematic world interaction and knowledge creation.

What is a model?

A model is a pattern, plan, representation (especially in miniature), or description designed to show the main object or workings of an object, system, or concept.

A model may refer to specific abstractions, concepts, and theories. Examples of models are:

- predictive formulas;
- causal models, i.e. abstract models that use cause and effect logic;
- mathematical models, i.e. abstract models that use mathematical language;
- economic models, i.e. theoretical constructs and their relations, representing economic processes;
- macroeconomic models, i.e. economic models representing a national or regional economy;
- business models, i.e. frameworks expressing the business logic of a firm;
- a meta-model, i.e. a model of a model;
- a computer model, i.e. a computer program which attempts to emulate an abstract model or theory of a particular part of the world;
- a data model, i.e. a description of the structure of a database;
- a physical model, i.e. a physical representation of an object like a prototype;
- solid models, representing unambiguous representations of the solid parts of an object;
- a scale model or a replica or prototype of an object;
- a 3D model, i.e. a 3D polygonal representation of an object, usually displayed with a computer; and
- a qualitative model, i.e. an abstract model that uses formal logic.

This chapter specifically studies mathematical and quantitative models as key model approaches for management decision making. This means that I do not go further into other possible objectives of modeling, like theory formation or scientific theory testing. This choice also has several consequences. In management decision making, most problems are not of a purely quantitative or qualitative nature. Besides, even if this is the case, most real-life problems are too complicated to cover all related variables and possible outcomes in one model. Therefore, most models are by definition simplifications of reality. This is also somewhat true for scientific modeling, but in the context of management we have to consider time pressure in the process of decision making, which gives an extra emphasis in deciding on a specific focus, without being able to fully account for each choice made. Instead of trying to create the "perfect" model of reality, Hammond *et al.* (1999) prefer a more practical approach to decision making by using their so-called PrOACT approach. According to Hammond *et al.*, even the most complex problems can be analyzed and resolved by considering the following four basic elements:

- Problem
    - Work on the right decision problem.
    - What must you decide?
    - Is it which car to buy or whether to buy one at all?
    - How should the problem be framed, i.e. formulated?
    - The way the problem is being framed can make all the difference.
    - Avoid unwarranted assumptions and option-limited prejudices.

- Objectives
    - Specify your objectives.
    - Your decision should get you where you want to go.
    - A decision is a means to an end.
    - Which of your interests, values, concerns, fears, and aspirations are most relevant to achieving your goal?
    - Thinking through your objectives will give direction to your decision making.

- Alternatives
    - Create imaginative alternatives.
    - Your alternatives should represent the different courses of action you have to choose from.
    - Without alternatives you wouldn't be facing a decision.
    - Have you considered all relevant alternatives?
    - Remember: your decision cannot be better than your best alternative.

- Consequences
    - Understand the consequences.
    - How well do the consequences satisfy your objectives?
    - Assessing frankly the consequences of each alternative will help you to identify those that best meet all your objectives.

- Trade-offs, i.e. the actual decision making by balancing the importance of the objectives, alternatives, and their consequences.

Within this framework, several qualitative as well as quantitative models may be used. Imagine you want to select a customer relationship management software package with functionalities that optimally match your company's needs. You then may develop a multifactor analysis when comparing the functionalities of these different software packages (when looking at alternative solutions) and may use a quantitative model for calculating the return on investment on alternative software packages (when looking at consequences). Or you may develop a decision tree in an earlier decision stage focusing on whether or not you would need a customer relationship management software package at all.

Hammond *et al.* (1999) also pay attention to problem-solving elements like uncertainty, risk tolerance, and linked decisions that are beyond the scope of this book. Figure 3.2 gives a summary of the Leibnizian epistemology in the context of management decision making. The emulation of reasoning in this figure is the calculation and logic mechanisms that are stored and may be processed by spreadsheets.

Mathematical (quantitative) models

A mathematical model is an abstract model that uses mathematical language to describe a system. Mathematical models can be classified in some of the following ways:

- *Linear versus nonlinear*. Mathematical models are usually composed of variables, which are abstractions of quantities of interest in the described systems, and operators that act on these variables, which can be algebraic operators, functions, differential operators, etc. If all the operators in a mathematical model present linearity, the resulting mathematical model is defined as linear. A model is considered to be nonlinear otherwise. Nonlinearity, even in fairly simple systems, is often associated with phenomena such as chaos and irreversibility. Although there are exceptions, nonlinear systems and models tend to be more difficult to study than linear ones. A common approach to nonlinear problems is linearization, but this can be problematic if one is trying to study aspects such as irreversibility which are strongly tied to nonlinearity.
- *Deterministic versus probabilistic* (stochastic). A deterministic model is one in which every set of variable states is uniquely determined by parameters in the model and by sets of previous states of these variables. Therefore, deterministic models perform the same way for a given set of initial conditions. Conversely, in a stochastic model, randomness is present, and variable states are not described by unique values, but rather by probability distributions.
- *Static versus dynamic*. A static model does not account for the element of time, while a dynamic model does. Dynamic models typically are represented with difference equations or differential equations.
- Mathematical modeling problems are often classified into *black-box* or *white-box models*, according to how much a priori information is available of the system. A black-box model is a system by which there is no a priori information available. A white-box model (also called glass box or clear box) is a system where all necessary information is available. Practically all systems are somewhere between the black-box and white-box models, so this concept only works as an intuitive guide for modeling. Sometimes it is useful to incorporate subjective

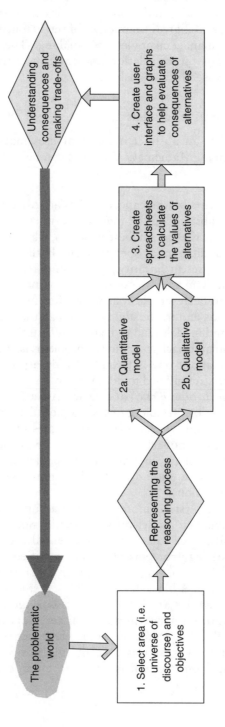

Figure 3.2 Leibnizian epistemology and management decision making.

information into a mathematical model. This can be done based on intuition, experience, or expert opinion, or based on convenience of mathematical form. In general, model complexity involves a trade-off between simplicity and accuracy of the model. *Occam's Razor* is a principle particularly relevant to modeling, the essential idea being that among models with roughly equal predictive power the simplest one is the most desirable. While added complexity usually improves the fit of a model, it can also make the model difficult to understand and work with, and pose computational problems, including numerical instability. Philosopher of science Thomas Kuhn (1970) argues that, as science progresses, explanations tend to become more complex before a paradigm shift offers radical simplification.

As an example, when modeling the flight of an aircraft, we could embed each mechanical part of the aircraft into our model and would thus acquire an almost white-box model of the system. However, the computational cost of adding such a huge amount of detail would effectively inhibit the usage of such a model. Additionally, the uncertainty would increase due to an overly complex system, because each separate part induces some amount of variance into the model. It is therefore usually appropriate to make some approximations to reduce the model to a sensible size. Engineers often can accept some approximations in order to get a more robust and simple model. For example, Newton's classical mechanics is an approximated model of the real world. Still, Newton's model is quite sufficient for most everyday situations, i.e. as long as particle speeds are well below the speed of light, and we study macro-particles only.

Developing quantitative models using MS-Excel

With a tool like Microsoft Excel, quantitative models can be built, simple as well as complex ones. Although some people see Excel as nothing more than an advanced calculator, it does enable people to develop and design informative quantitative models. Basically, compared to databases, a spreadsheet is exactly the same as a table, i.e. consists of columns which are the same as attributes in the database, and rows which consist of the instances of a database. MS-Excel enables us to manage several spreadsheet pages in one book, and each spreadsheet page consists of a table. The data integrity between the tables in a spreadsheet can be managed by copying the data between pages or creating referential links between cells of different tables. This, though, is a rather clumsy process, and therefore we do not see spreadsheets as an alternative for databases, which enable integrity between tables via data models.

As stated before, models aim at efficient ways of explaining or predicting phenomena, and they do this by relating dependent and independent variables via causalities. Causal (note that causality is a key concept for Leibniz) models can be expressed by relating independent and dependent variables by directional graphs which show the direction and strength of the causality and also whether it is positive or negative (by a "+" sign or "−" sign in the graph). MS-Visio has several ways of making these charts (e.g. its Block Diagram/Basic Diagram option has rectangles that can be used for expressing variables and it has dynamic connectors for expressing causal graphs). An example of a causal model is given in Figure 3.3.

These causalities may have certain transformation rules to transform the value of an independent variable into the value of a dependent variable. These variables (also named parameters in mathematics or attributes in databases) are mostly represented in spreadsheets via their columns. For the systematic development of spreadsheets one therefore needs the specification of dependent variable(s), independent variable(s), causalities as transformation rules mostly expressed in formulas, and the instances one is going to review. Table 3.1 gives an overview of these concepts, and relates them with the key concepts on databases.

Imagine that you are looking for a new car. After checking some Internet sites and talking to some people, you find four different cars (i.e. four alternatives which will be the instances you are going to compare). Which of these cars is the best one for you? This question implies that there is some kind of dependent variable, which we could name "utility," and the highest utility giver is of course the best alternative. Finding the independent variables and how intensely (i.e. formulas) they influence your dependent variable (utility) is the key to solving this decision problem. Following the PrOACT method, we solve this problem as follows:

1   First you have to describe the *problem*. The problem here is that you want to select the best car for you to buy. This is by way of a quite substantial narrowing of a personal transportation problem, because it excludes non-car alternatives (like public transportation, motor bikes, or bicycles).

2   Then you have to look at the objectives and their *decision criteria*. What criteria do you want to use to select the best alternative? The decision criteria are the independent variables that influence your utility. You could make an overview of decision criteria like purchase costs, fuel consumption, level of luxury, car design, safety, amortization costs, and operating reliability (i.e. negative of breakdowns).

3   Next, you have to decide how *important* these criteria are, for example, on a 1 (not important) to 10 (very important) scale, by which you specify the causality or contributions of these independent variables on your

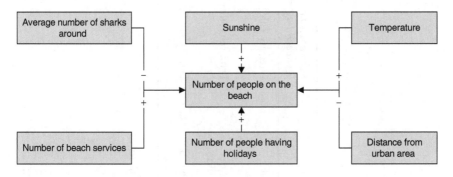

Figure 3.3 A causal model explaining the number of people on a beach.

perceived utility. See Table 3.2. (We leave the expression of these relations via a causal Visio model to the reader.) Of course, you also have to make a list of the *alternatives* (the instances) available, e.g. the BMW Mini, Seat Arosa, Citroen C2, Volkswagen Lupo GTI, and Toyota Aygo. Note that we may have incomplete alternatives, but visiting all the dealers to view all possibly relevant alternatives simply will take too much time.

4   The next step is to score the different alternatives, also on a 1 (not important) to 10 (very important) scale, as done in Table 3.3.

5   Scoring is a personal affair, but always needs the handling of trade-offs between the different decision criteria. In our example it seems the person who scored the alternatives was fairly money conscious. (Another person may score in a different way and have a different "winning car" as a consequence.) For each car, we now have to multiply the score with the "importance scales" of each criterion, by which we calculate the impact of the independent variables on the dependent variable (utility). After adding up all the scores, you get the total utility score per car, as present in Table 3.4. The results can be shown graphically too, as done in Figure 3.4.

The resultant winner of this process is the Aygo. This is an easy and straightforward method, but it is certainly not a perfect one. Can you think of improvements?

Before closing this subsection, it is important to note that the decision problem we used as an example is also known as a *multi-criteria decision problem,* and we need to refer to the decision science literature (like the journals of *Multi-Criteria Decision Analysis* and *Decision Sciences*) for more information on these kinds of problems.

Table. 3.1 Spreadsheet components and related terms

Spreadsheet terms	*Spreadsheet (page)*	*Row*	*Column 2*	*Column 3*	*Formula*	*Data equivalence (between pages)*
Related terms in databases	Table	Instance	Attribute	Attribute	Formula	Integrity rule
Related terms in social science	File, sample, or population	Unit	Independent variable	Dependent variable	Causality, correlation, slope	Data reliability
Related terms in mathematics	Sample or population	Unit or instance	Parameter	Parameter	Formula, function, operator	Data reliability

Note
One may also put the attributes in the rows and the instances in the columns, when just a few instances need to be reviewed.

Table 3.2 A possible rating of car selection criteria

Criterion	Importance (i.e. causal relation to your utility)
Low purchase costs	8.5
Low fuel consumption	5
Luxury	7
Design	7.8
Safety	6
Low amortization	7
Reliability	8

Table 3.3 A spreadsheet page of alternatives

	Mini	Arosa	C2	Lupo GTI	Aygo
Low purchase costs	1.5	8	6	4	7
Low fuel consumption	5	7	7	5	9
Luxury	9	5	7	7	5
Design	9	7.5	7.5	7.6	6
Safety	8	6.5	7	6.5	6
Low amortization	8.5	8	6	8	9
Reliability	7.8	7.2	7.4	7	9.5

Table 3.4 A spreadsheet of alternatives and objectives

Alternatives →		Mini	Arosa	C2	Lupo GTI	Aygo
Objectives ↓	Importance					
Low purchase costs	9	13	68	51	34	60
Low fuel consumption	5	25	35	35	25	45
Luxury	7	63	35	49	49	35
Design	8	70	59	59	59	47
Safety	6	48	39	42	39	36
Low amortization	7	60	56	42	56	63
Reliability	8	62	58	59	56	76
	Total:	341	350	337	318	362

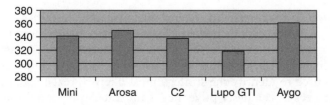

Figure 3.4 A graphical presentation of consequences produced with MS-Excel.

Qualitative models

Previously we focused on quantitative models. Here we look more specifically at qualitative models and especially at one type of qualitative model: decision charts.

Qualitative modeling based on *logic* involves the following ideas. Propositions are simple statements such as "rich people are happy, poor people are unhappy". Propositions can be true or false, and negation of a proposition transforms truth into falsity, or falsity into truth. Compound statements are formed when two or more propositions are placed in disjunction or conjunction, signified in English by the words *or* (or *nor*) and *and* (or *but*). Compound statements are true if all their component propositions are true, and compound statements are false if all their component propositions are false. Disjunction of true and false propositions yields a compound statement that is true, whereas conjunction of true and false propositions yields a compound statement that is false. These definitions are sufficient for logical analyses, but a supplementary definition is useful: the conditional "P implies Q" or "if P then Q" means that, whenever proposition P is true, proposition Q is true also, but when P is false, Q may be either true or false. In general, qualitative models describe systematic structures and processes, and developing qualitative models aids in interpreting nebulous phenomena.

Compared to quantitative models, qualitative models thus have several limitations. One key limitation is that qualitative models do not use *continuous* variables, but use *discrete* ones, i.e. variables for a few values, often only two, and clear cut-offs between these values. This is often the case with variables such as gender, nationality, type of car, rich versus poor, and lower or higher educated. Such nominal or ordinal classifications are important for decision making, because often people cannot easily choose all possible imaginary options. For instance, while delivering someone a German passport, you cannot simply give this person it only for one half. An interesting question may be if this person is allowed to have other nations' passports at the same time, but still the real world is not always that discrete. This makes qualitative modeling often very complex. For instance, the case of gender and the problems of a clear classification between male or female have been debated many times in the context of athletics. Many laws use discrete logic, and consequently lawyers have a hard job in resolving cases which are not so easy to classify.

Three types of qualitative modeling can be distinguished:

1   *Decision trees/charts.* In operations research, specifically decision analysis, a decision tree (or tree diagram) is a decision support tool that uses a graph or model of decisions and their possible consequences, including chance-event outcomes, resource costs, and utility. A decision tree is used to identify the strategy most likely to reach a goal. Another use of trees is as a descriptive means for calculating conditional probabilities. Decision trees are formulated as "if . . . then" statements, i.e. the checking of a condition, which may be true or false, and based on

this conclusion a consequence is drawn. Figure 3.5 gives an example of a decision tree. The figure shows the rules that will apply for providing people with a parking allowance, given the scarcity of parking space around an office, and a policy of a parking place owner to reduce the number of people using the parking space.

2   Figure 3.6 gives a decision chart that may help people to diagnose loan problems. As seen, the concept of a decision chart is essentially the same as a decision tree, though its representation is done more in natural language as a question–answer–consequence flow, allowing non-experts to easily diagnose themselves. Such decision charts can be presented in many ways by MS-Visio techniques. What you need are different objects for representing "start," "finish" (i.e. consequences), question objects, arrows, and answer objects. These objects and arrows thus form a representation language or modeling language for decision charts.

3   *Decision table.* A concept strongly related to the decision tree and decision chart concept is the decision table. In decision tables, the possible "answers" are in the decision tree and chart binary, i.e. "Yes" or "No." Certain combinations fit with one consequence represented by an "X." Table 3.5 is an example of a "discount rate decision table". In everyday language, the table implies that, when someone orders less than 50 units, pays cash on delivery, but does not buy at a wholesale outlet, then this person should get a discount of 4 percent. Decision tables are very useful for documenting decision rules and delivering this information to programmers of transaction processing systems (like many e-commerce and bureaucratic rule-processing systems).

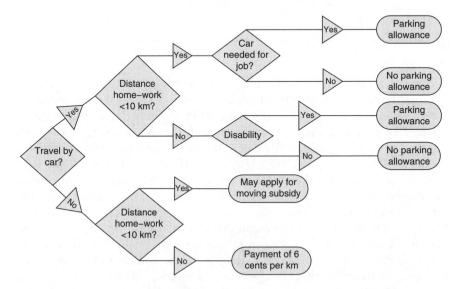

Figure 3.5 An example of a decision tree related to providing parking allowances and travel budgets (created by MS-Visio's basic flow chart option).

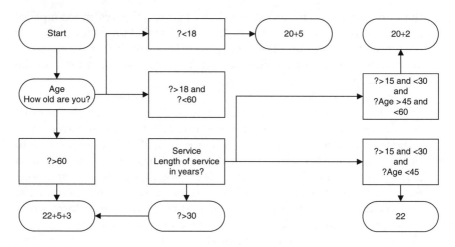

Figure 3.6 A decision chart.

Table 3.5 A decision table for discount percent allocation

Conditions	Less than 50 units ordered	Y	Y	Y	Y	N	N	N	N
	Cash on delivery	Y	Y	N	N	Y	Y	N	N
	Wholesale outlet	Y	N	Y	N	Y	N	Y	N
Consequences	Discount rate 0%				X				
	Discount rate 2%		X	X					X
	Discount rate 4%	X					X	X	
	Discount rate 6%						X		

Because it is often difficult to classify instances by discrete variables, *fuzzy logic* has been introduced. Fuzzy logic is derived from fuzzy set theory dealing with reasoning that is approximate rather than precisely deduced from classical predicate logic. It can be thought of as the application side of fuzzy set theory dealing with well-thought-out real world expert values for a complex problem (Klir and Yuan, 1995). Degrees of truth are often confused with probabilities. However, they are distinct conceptually; fuzzy truth represents membership in vaguely defined sets, not likelihood of some event or condition. For example, if a 100-ml glass contains 30 ml of water, then, for two fuzzy sets, Empty and Full, one might define the glass as being 0.7 empty and 0.3 full. Note that the concept of emptiness is subjective and thus depends on the observer or designer. Another designer might equally well design a set membership function where the glass would be considered full for all values down to 50 ml. A probabilistic setting would first define a scalar variable for the fullness of the glass and, second, conditional distributions describing the probability that someone would call the glass full given a specific fullness level. Note that the conditioning can be achieved by having a specific observer who randomly selects the label for the glass, a distribution over deterministic observers, or both. While fuzzy logic avoids talking about randomness in this context, this simplification at the same time obscures what is exactly meant by the statement "the glass is 0.3 full." Fuzzy logic allows for set membership values to range (inclusively) between 0 and 1, and, in its linguistic form, imprecise concepts like "slightly," "quite," and "very." Specifically, it allows partial membership in a set. Fuzzy logic is controversial in some circles, and is rejected by some control engineers and by most statisticians who hold that probability is the only rigorous mathematical description of uncertainty.

Although MS-Visio does not support logical consistency checking, you can easily create decision trees like the one shown in Figure 3.5 by using the standard "Basic flow chart" option of MS-Visio. If you do not know MS-Visio too well, you could go through its tutorial.[2] In less than an hour you will get the basics behind this great tool. Decision rules can be implemented in spreadsheets by using, for example, the IF, SUMIF, and MAX formula option in MS-Excel.[3] For advanced use of MS-Excel, we highly recommend reading Tennent and Friend (2005).

Reflective practice

You may want to say that, if a model is a simplification of reality, it is not practical and useful at all. As a defense for models, though, I would argue that simplification makes complex issues manageable, but of course the simplification must add value. Keep it as simple as possible (Occam's Razor)! You can apply the idea of modeling to the management of many everyday decision problems.

A first example of such an everyday problem is the planning of your personal income, spending, and savings. Try, for instance, to put your income, spending, and savings of a week, a month, and a full year into an MS-Excel spreadsheet. Next, extrapolate this spreadsheet over the next four years. Also apply some "if . . . then" calculations, like buying a new car in Year 2, getting a salary raise of 5 percent each year, or paying for an apartment and the extra cost of living for your daughter who starts university in Year 3.

Here is another example: John gets a new job in a town 100 kilometers from the place he lives. His wife, though, has a very good job at the moment and does not want to move. His new boss understands the problem, and offers John 15 cents per kilometer compensation. John, therefore, decides to drive each day the 200 kilometers, but his old car will not be of assistance with this. He now considers buying a new BMW 118i made in 2008 costing 38,000 euros, using 5 liters of fuel per 100 kilometers and with maintenance costs of 10 cents per kilometer. Alternatively, he considers buying an older BMW 118i from 2004, costing him 18,000 euros, using 7.2 liters of fuel per 100 kilometers and with maintenance costs of 18 cents per kilometer. Assume that the fuel price in the first year is 1.53 per liter, 1.75 in the second year, 1.93 in the third year, and 2.15 in the fourth. John expects to sell the new BMW for 15,000 euros after Year 4 and the older version for 8,000 euros after four years. He needs a full loan at an 8 percent interest rate. Calculate during the period of four years what the best choice is for John economically. Assume that his boss will probably not offer more than 15 cents during this period.

A third example: now you are going to *model* a problem, i.e. select the variables and formulas that should be placed in the spreadsheet. An example is the production and publishing of a novel. And for a qualitative case, on the delivery of parking permissions at a parking lot with insufficient space for all car owners. First make a causal model and then implement the rules on the spreadsheet and decision chart or tree.

Also discuss the issues with your virtual study group and make two reports, one on how to make quantitative models and how to implement them in MS-Excel, and one on making qualitative decision models by MS-Visio.

Further reading

Elementary further reading

Kroenke, D. M. (2008) *Experiencing Management Information Systems*. Upper Saddle River, NJ: Pearson Prentice Hall, especially pp. 92–114, 329–342, and 483–492.

On Leibniz

Churchman, C. W. (1971) *The Design of Inquiring Systems: Basic Concepts of Systems and Organization*. New York: Basic Books.

Look, B. C. (2008) "Gottfried Wilhelm Leibniz," in E. N. Zalta (ed.) *The Stanford Encyclopedia of Philosophy* (Spring 2008 Edition), http://plato.stanford.edu/archives/spr2008/entries/leibniz; accessed May, 2008.

On qualitative decision modeling

Spenser, C. (2007) "Drawing on your knowledge with VisiRule," *IEEE Potentials*, Jan./Feb.: 20–25.

On decision making and problem solving

Hammond, J., Keeny, R., and Raiffa, H. (1999) *Smart Choices—A Practical Guide to Making Better Life Decisions*. Boston, MA: Harvard Business School Press.

On spreadsheets and (business) modeling

To get started with MS-Excel: http://office.microsoft.com/training/training.aspx?AssetID=RC100766511033

Advanced spreadsheet use: Tennent, J. and Friend, G. (2005) *Guide to Business Modeling*. London: Profile Books.

On MS-Visio

The link http://office.microsoft.com/en-us/visio/HA102144941033.aspx has concise and very useful beginners' instructions.

On fuzzy logic

Klir, G. and Yuan, B. (1995) *Fuzzy Sets and Fuzzy Logic: Theory and Applications*. Upper Saddle River, NJ: Prentice Hall.

4 The Kantian view and multiple perspectives

Introduction to the philosophy of Immanuel Kant

Kant[1]

Immanuel Kant was an eighteenth-century German philosopher. He is regarded as one of the most influential thinkers of modern Europe and of the late Enlightenment. He was baptized as "Emanuel" but later changed his name to "Immanuel" after he learned Hebrew. He spent his entire life in and around his hometown, never traveling more than a hundred miles from Königsberg. In his youth, Kant was a solid, albeit unspectacular, student. He was raised in a pietist household that stressed intense religious devotion, personal humility, and a literal interpretation of the Bible. Consequently, Kant received a stern education—strict, punitive, and disciplinary—that favored Latin and religious instruction over mathematics and science.

Kant defined the Enlightenment in the essay "Answering the Question: What is Enlightenment?" as an age shaped by the motto "Dare to know." This involved thinking autonomously, free of the dictates of external authority. Kant's work served as a bridge between the Rationalist and Empiricist traditions of the eighteenth century. He had a decisive impact on the Romantic and German Idealist philosophies of the nineteenth century. The foundations of what Kant called his *critical philosophy* place the active, rational human subject at the center of the cognitive and moral worlds. With regard to knowledge, Kant argued that the rational order of the world as known by science could never be accounted for merely by the fortuitous accumulation of sense perceptions, i.e. Locke's empiricism. Instead, rational order is the product of the rule-based activity of "synthesis." This consists of conceptual unification and integration carried out by the mind through concepts or the "categories of the understanding" operating on the perceptual manifold within space and time, which are not concepts, but forms of sensibility that are a priori necessary conditions for any possible experience. Space and time are two of these fundamental a prioris for natural sciences (but possibly for most other sciences as well), and space and time properties can be further expressed in geometric and mathematic language. These a prioris are given to mankind, and without them people will not be able to perceive reality (Churchman, 1971: 145). Thus the objective order of nature and the causal necessity that operates within it are dependent upon the mind and its "innate" (to re-use Leibniz's term here) a prioris. There is wide disagreement among Kant scholars on the correct interpretation of this train of thought. The "two-world" interpretation regards Kant's position as a statement of epistemological limitation, that we are never able to transcend the bounds of our own mind, meaning that we cannot access the "thing-in-itself." Kant, however, also speaks of the "thing-in-itself" or transcendental object as a product of the (human) understanding as it attempts to conceive of objects in abstraction from the conditions of sensibility. Following this thought, some interpreters have argued that the "thing-in-itself" does not represent a separate ontological domain but simply is a way of considering objects by means of the understanding alone—this is known as the two-aspect view. Consequently, Kant is not a pure rationalist, who would base *all* understanding on innate human capabilities alone, but emphasizes the reciprocity of sensations and concepts. According to Churchman (1971), we should understand this as the limitations of rationality and deduction in explaining the world, and the possibility of inquiring systems to sense facts and experiences that are not fully under control of existing theories and nomological networks. This capability of confronting existing knowledge with inconsistent observation and facts is essential for human progress and scientific learning.

With regard to morality, Kant argued that the source of the good lies not in anything outside the human subject, either in nature or given by God, but rather only the good *will* itself. A good will is one that acts from duty in accordance with the universal moral law that the autonomous human being freely gives itself. This law obliges one to treat *humanity*—understood as rational agency, and represented through oneself as well as others—*as an end in itself* rather than (merely) as means.

Kant's theses—that the mind itself necessarily makes a constitutive contribution to its knowledge, that this contribution is transcendental rather than psychological, that philosophy involves self-critical activity, that morality is rooted in human freedom, and that to act autonomously is to act according to rational moral principles—have all had a lasting effect on subsequent philosophers.

Kant defines his theory of perception in his work *The Critique of Pure Reason* (1781). Kant maintains that our understanding of the external world has its foundations not merely in experience, but in *both experience and a priori concepts*—thus offering a non-empiricist critique of rationalist philosophy, which is what he and others referred to as his "Copernican revolution." The a priori concepts can be of an analytic or synthetic kind:

1   *Analytic a prioris* are propositions whose predicate concept is contained in its subject concept, e.g. "All bachelors are unmarried," or,

"All bodies take up space." Thus, analytic propositions are true by nature of the meaning of the words involved in the sentence—we require no further knowledge than a grasp of the language to understand such propositions.

2 *Synthetic a prioris* are propositions whose predicate concept is not contained in its subject concept, e.g. "All bachelors are happy," or, "All bodies have mass." Thus, synthetic statements are those that tell us something about the world. Synthetic statements are true or false because their meaning transcends the content of the language used. In this instance, mass is not a necessary predicate to the body; until we are told the heaviness of the body we do not know that it has mass. In this case, experience of the body is required before its heaviness becomes clear. Kant claims that elementary mathematics, like arithmetic, consists of synthetic a prioris. Here Kant posits that it is in fact possible to have knowledge of the world that is not derived from empirical experience, but that experience depends on certain necessary conditions—which he calls a priori forms—and that these conditions hold true for the world. In so doing, his main claims in the "Transcendental Aesthetic" are that mathematic judgments are synthetic a prioris, i.e. they are *necessary conditions* for experience.

This means also that Kant believes that a priori, people are able to make empirical observations, which he names a posteriori propositions. A posteriori propositions thus are statements about our world based on experience and observation (using the a priori of course). This also implies that much of the concepts we use for acquiring and organizing data (like data models and calculation models) are a priori propositions and that the data in our databases and the outcomes of our spreadsheet calculations are a posteriori propositions.

Consequences for information management

A key point here for information management is that people are free to take their own view of the world, and consequently this freedom will allow people to take different views even about the same phenomena. So as "consumers" of models of the world, we have to understand why people have this view, what the view really entails, and how different views can help in realizing deeper or better views of the world. This seems to be in conflict with the Lockean attempts to converge to one single community using the same universe of discourse description. It also seems to be in conflict with Leibnizian attempts to find the one single best model of the world. Kant would argue that one can see one phenomenon from multiple perspectives. Nevertheless, people will probably share sufficient a priori concepts so that they can understand each other and thus become suppliers of complementary information. The development of insights from Locke and Leibniz to Kant is illustrated in Figure 4.1.

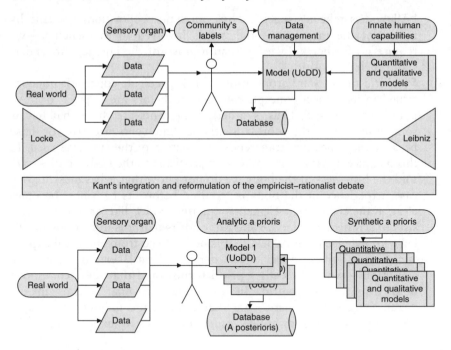

Figure 4.1 Kant's additions to the theories of Locke and Leibniz.

Figure 4.1 indicates that Kant proposes to more precisely denote Locke's labels as analytic and synthetic propositions, and also describes Leibniz's logic and causality concept as synthetic a prioris. The observations and data that are enabled by the a priori propositions consist of a posteriori propositions and may be stored in a database. The distinction of analytic and synthetic propositions has been mentioned in the previous discussion of databases, where attributes and relationships have been identified as the same type of distinction. When using formulas in MS-Excel for calculations, most of them are *synthetic* a prioris. On the other hand, statistics as descriptions of actual facts are a posterioris. We need synthetic a prioris to understand many business and organizational phenomena, but *many business and organization concepts are synthetic a prioris*. For instance, the idea that organizations have a strategy, structure, and process are key concepts without experiential basis, but a priori true, because if a unit does not have a process, strategy, and structure we may not call it an organization. Much of our understanding of organizations, though, additionally requires a combination of observations and reasoning by free people who contribute their view of the world consisting also of synthetic a posterioris. Table 4.1 summarizes the key terms and gives examples.

Table 4.1 Kant's propositions, examples, and importance

	A priori propositions	A posteriori propositions
Analytic	Example: All bachelors are unmarried. Important for data definitions and semantic standardization of concepts.	
Synthetic	Example: Bachelors can be happy. 5+7=12. Important for managing relations between data.	Example: 60% of bachelors are happy; 20% of them are unhappy; 20% are neither happy nor unhappy. Important for registering empirical facts.

The consequences for information management can be summarized as follows:

1   Empiricism is correct in the sense that we do need sensory mechanisms and abilities to carefully manage data.
2   Rationalism is correct as well, as we need good innate concepts for making sense (i.e. knowledge) of our data.
3   Additionally, there may be many competing data sources and models of the same reality. We need ways of handling this diversity in a constructive way by rejecting incorrect ones and integrating the correct ones to a more profound view of reality.
4   Kant did not have information-age software tools for modeling and documenting the many models we need to understand a phenomenon. We will discuss the opportunities of MS-Visio for this purpose later in this chapter.
5   These modeling tools help describe and document organizational a prioris such as organizational rules, organization structures, and organization processes.
6   Additionally, today we have enterprise software packages available which aim at integrating different models of the same reality.
7   Some key a prioris used in modeling organizations and business processes are, in addition to Kant's time (when) and space (where), the what, how, who, and why (Sowa and Zachman, 1992).

Figure 4.2 summarizes the Kantian model for information management.

Multi-perspective modeling

For a phenomenon to be represented in a manner that is accurate, complete, embedded in its context, and yet comprehensible, *multi-perspective modeling*

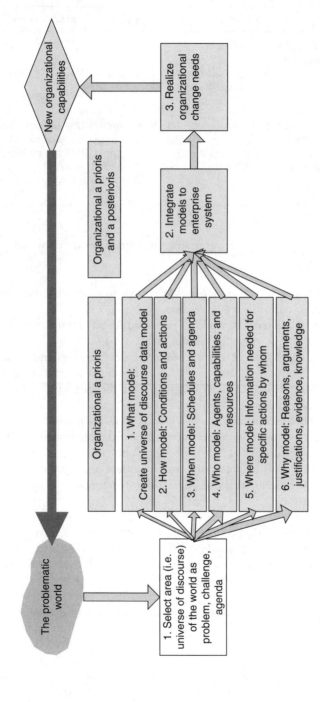

Figure 4.2 A model of the Kantian epistemology and information management.

is required. Each of these models takes a different viewpoint. The different viewpoints can be thought of as different managers' views on the organization: for example, an operations manager might view the organization as a user, consumer, and producer of resources, while a personnel manager might view the organization as a network of interactions between agents. Models consist of nodes (boxes, circles, diamonds, etc.), which represent objects of the universe of discourse, and arcs (arrows, lines), which represent relationships between these objects (see Chapter 2). The diagram formats may (and probably should) differ between perspectives, but all knowledge items are drawn from a single underlying repository.

Sowa and Zachman (1992) have proposed to use the following perspectives for information systems modeling, which are relevant too for information management: *how* a process is carried out, *who* does it, *what* information is needed, *where* that information comes from, *when* each activity must be carried out, and (less explicitly) *why* the process is performed. These perspectives are not simply different views held by different actors, but refer to six a priori forms for business and organization. Of course, more a priori forms could be identified, but the six mentioned here have been very influential in the development of modern enterprise models (see, for example, Scheer, 1998), and therefore need special attention here. Table 4.2 gives more details on the contents of these perspectives.

Table 4.2 Descriptions of information management perspectives

Perspective	Description
What	Declarative knowledge about things as opposed to procedural knowledge about actions. What knowledge encompasses: concepts, physical objects, and states. It also includes knowledge about classifications or categorizations of those states.
How	Knowledge about actions and events. It includes knowledge about which actions are required if certain events occur, which actions will achieve certain states, and the required or preferred ordering of actions.
When	When actions or events happen, or should happen; it is knowledge about the controls needed on timing and ordering of events.
Who	The agents (human or automated) that carry out each action; their capabilities and authority to carry out particular actions.
Where	Where knowledge is needed and where it originates from—communication and input/output knowledge.
Why	Rationale: reasons, arguments, empirical studies, and justification for things that are done and the way they are done.

Based on Kingston and MacIntosh (2000) and Sowa and Zachman (1992).

Table 4.3 The Zachman framework

	Data (what)	Function (how)	Network (where)	People (who)	Time (when)	Motivation (why)
Objectives/scope (textual)	List of things important to the business	List of processes the business performs	List of locations in which the business operates	List of organizations important to the business	List of events significant to the business	List of business goals/strategies
Enterprise (conceptual)	Semantic model	Business process model	Business legacy systems	Work flow model	Master schedule	Business plan
System (logical)	Logical data model	Application architecture	Distributed systems architecture	Human interface architecture	Processing structure	Business rule model
Technology contrained (physical)	Physical data model	System design	System architecture	Presentation architecture	Control structure	Rule design
Detailed representation (out-of-context)	Data description	Programs	Network architecture	Security architecture	Tuning description	Rule specification
Functioning enterprise	Data	Function	Network	Organization	Schedule	Strategy

Based on Sowa and Zachman (1992).

The framework (also called the "Zachman framework") has six columns representing *who, what, how, when, where,* and *why* perspectives on knowledge, and six rows representing different levels of abstraction (see Table 4.3). Sowa and Zachman illustrate the different levels of abstraction using examples from the design and construction of a building, starting from the "scope" level (which takes a "ballpark" view on the building which is primarily the concern of the architect, and may represent the gross sizing, shape, and spatial relationships as well as the mutual understanding between the architect and owner), going through the "enterprise" level (primarily the concern of the owner, representing the final building as seen by the owner, and floor plans, based on the architect's drawings), and on through three other levels (the "system" level, the "technology constrained" level, and the "detailed representation" level, respectively, which are the concerns of the designer, the builder, and the sub-contractor) before arriving at the "functioning enterprise" level (in this example, the actual building). Sowa and Zachman describe this framework as a simple, logical structure of descriptive representations for identifying "models" that are the basis for designing the enterprise and for building the enterprise's systems. The higher levels of abstraction (the top two rows) represent the organizational context and the enterprise. The lower-level models provide a comprehensive design specification for enterprise systems.

Using MS-Visio for multi-perspective modeling

There is not enough space in this book for detailed explanations of multi-perspective models showing all six perspectives at all six levels of abstraction. Instead, we will look at all the perspectives at one level of abstraction only, the enterprise—also named the conceptual level—using project management as an example.

The how *perspective: Project management protocol*

The enterprise level of the *how* should create a single entity; in this case, the entity being created is a consulting firm's client solution with a subsequent implementation plan. In this domain, the *how* knowledge can be represented by a protocol. A protocol gives a step-by-step guide for carrying out a certain specialized procedure, drawing on all (and only) the business experience and other knowledge relevant to that procedure. The motivation behind developing protocols is to capture and represent "best practice."

A common way of quickly starting up projects is to reuse common best practices, which may be described by Figure 4.3 and the following:

1   A *plan,* i.e. a sequence of sub-tasks or components, needs to be carried out to achieve an objective, such as a project's assessment of the client's existing IT portfolio in terms of strategic fit, costs, and consistency.

a The *how* model

b The *how* model specified for the IT assessment project

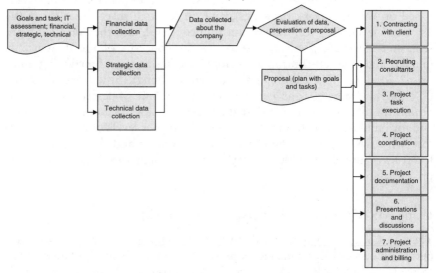

Figure 4.3 The four basic shapes for modeling the *how* using the MS-Visio workflow chart.

Plan components are usually ordered, to reflect temporal, logical, resource, or other constraints.

2   An *enquiry* or data collection is a task whose objective is to obtain an item of information that is needed in order to complete a procedure or take a decision. This task has several steps: (1) the specification of an enquiry, which includes a description of the information required; (2) data collection activities through interviews with responsible agents and surveys of the existing situation; and (3) documentation of the results in a (management) report.

3   A *decision* occurs at any point in a guideline or protocol when some sort of choice has to be made, such as a proposal to the client.

4   An *action* is a procedure that is to be enacted outside the computer system, typically by employees, such as the writing of reports, delivery of presentations, and moderation of discussions with key decision makers.

Figure 4.3b shows a portion of the protocol that will be used throughout this example: it guides project members through the decision on how to treat a specific client problem, in this case the assessment of a firm's IT portfolio on financial, strategic, and IT consistency criteria.

The where *perspective: Project communication*

The *where* perspective shows communication that is needed during a procedure. At the enterprise level of abstraction, communication is generally concerned with the transfer of information or artifacts between individuals or departments. In the example earlier, financial, strategy, and IT consultants must communicate on topics they share. The IT consultants, for instance, will deliver a description of the information systems and the infrastructure for these systems (i.e. the IT support organization, security services, data communication services, and development organization). These descriptions are shared with the strategy and financial consultants, who next can calculate costs and strategic contributions. The three consultant groups need a shared agenda to know the status of deliveries so that they can each plan their activities, and the project manager needs these data for status reporting to the client. The project manager also needs data concerning the delivered hours per function types, so that he or she can bill and check the project's consumption of the budget.

This information can be represented in an organization chart of the involved departments and a cross-functional flow chart which shows the division and interrelation of activities among the organizational departments. MS-Visio enables ways of drafting organization charts via its organization chart templates, as given in Figure 4.4.

The division of tasks and their interrelations can be drafted using MS-Visio cross-functional flow diagrams, as shown in Figure 4.5. Note the use of different objects or forms for documents, processes, tasks, data, and decisions, and columns for identifying responsible organizational units. These objects and their interlinkages, consisting of arrows, are a representation language for cross-functional flows.

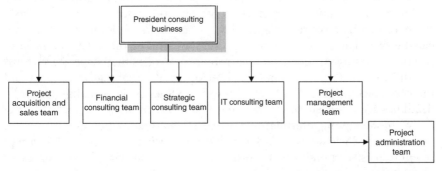

Figure 4.4 The "where" perspective—An organization chart using an MS-Visio organization chart template.

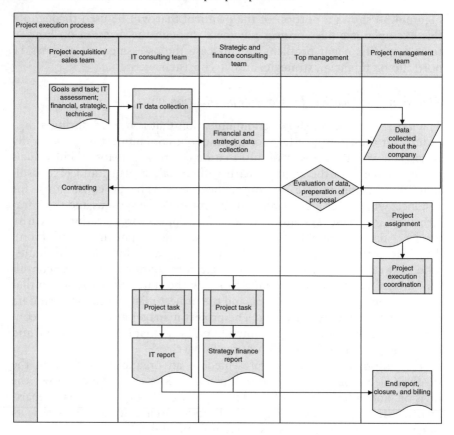

Figure 4.5 Cross-functional flow diagram using MS-Visio cross-flowchart templates.

The who *perspective: Participants and departments*

There is a need for the *who* perspective to represent the *capability* of agents, departments, or other role-players to perform certain actions and the *authority* that certain agents have to perform those actions or to use, consume, or modify resources (Figure 4.6). At an enterprise level of abstraction, capability and authority may be expressed by defining the *rights* and *responsibilities* of an agent. For example, project managers may have the right to assign employees on tasks implying both authority to change an artifact and the capability to do so, as well as responsibilities such as making sure the deadlines are achieved and sufficient quality is realized.

For modeling the interrelations between agents, activities, and resources, one can use MS-Visio's block diagram option, using rounded angles to represent actors, rectangles to represent activities, and triangles to represent resources. See Figure 4.6.

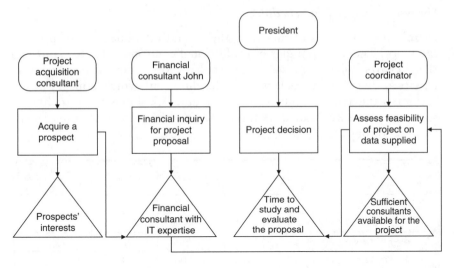

Figure 4.6 Capabilities, authorities, rights, and responsibilities of agents, modeled by MS-Visio block diagrams.

The what *perspective: Data, information, and resources*

The *what* perspective considers the *data* and *information* that are referred to and the *resources* that are used, consumed, modified, manipulated, or otherwise involved in the overall process. The enterprise level of the *what* perspective should contain data classes, which are sub-classes of global data classes; the relationships between classes can be defined using entity-relationship diagrams. In our example, data classes might include reports, presentations, and tasks; information represented in data classes might include results; and resources include the people, budgets, and possible external experts required. The resources may have associated constraints; for example, use of a consultant may require several weeks' notice, or scarce experts may not be available and thus consultants have to be hired externally.

The *what* perspective clearly identifies what is named an Entity Relationship Diagram (ERD) in Chapter 2 (see Figure 2.4). Because the modeling of the *what* is identical to the modeling of entity-relations as described in Chapter 2, we do not give them again here. Table 4.2 names the data model at the Enterprise level a "semantic" model, which implies that the model must be understandable in everyday language. The data model at the System level concerns only the formal logical representation of this semantic model (e.g. by focusing on cardinalities and 1:N or M:N relationships). These formal logical models can be "understood" by computer systems which are able to process these logical relations. Most ERD modeling techniques both cover the semantic and logical relation of data.

The when *perspective: Schedules*

There are many ways of modeling the when/time dimension of projects and work. The most popular in professional environments are Gantt and PERT charts, which are well supported by MS-Visio. Such charts give activities, inter-activity delays, and the duration (which appears at the bottom of the activity node in weeks). Figure 4.7 shows a Gantt chart of our case, where we defined six tasks and an ultimate delivery time for the proposal of one month.

ID	Task Name	Start	Finish	Duration	Feb 2008 3-2	10-2	17-2	24-2
1	Task1 IT data collection	4-2-2008	11-2-2008	1,2w	▭			
2	Task2 Strategic data collection	11-2-2008	18-2-2008	1,2w		▭		
3	Task3 Financial data collection	11-2-2008	18-2-2008	1,2w		▭		
4	Task4 Preparation of plan	18-2-2008	25-2-2008	1,2w			▭	
5	Task5 Management decision	25-2-2008	25-2-2008	2w			▯	
6	Task6 Contracting	26-2-2008	3-3-2008	1w				▭

Figure 4.7 A Gantt chart for preparing the proposal using the MS-Visio Project Schedule, Gantt option.

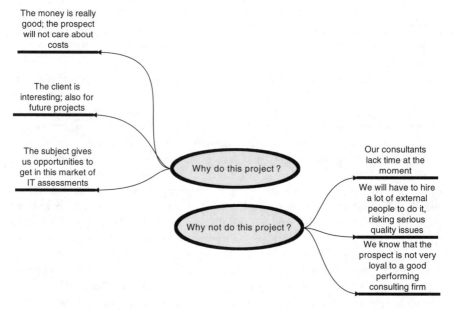

Figure 4.8 Using MS-Visio brainstorming to structure arguments to offer or not offer a project proposal to a client.

The why *perspective: Documents and evidence*

The *why* knowledge consists of evidence: published results, meta-studies, and expert opinions. The *why* knowledge may consist of all known articles published to date. These justifications can be represented in a rationale diagram, which can be created by, for example, MS-Visio's brainstorming options (see Figure 4.8).

Model integration and enterprise architectures

As stated before, Kant is not only important for his recognition of the freedom of individuals to see their world in the specific way they need, but also for the challenges he poses to people to find ways of integrating the resulting different views. In an organizational perspective this is complex, because, in addition to the different ways that are possible in modeling a same reality (e.g. project development), organizations have different departments and functions with different types of universes of discourse. We will not go into details here, but the reader can easily imagine the complexity of integrating the universes of discourse of operations managers, production managers, human resource managers, accountants, and controllers (just to mention a few typical functions in a manufacturing firm). Cross-functional modeling aims at integrating these universes of discourse in a single workflow. Currently so-called enterprise system vendors, like SAP and Oracle, aim to provide the information technological platform to let the different databases and applications (e.g. decision support systems) share relevant data and functionalities. These enterprise systems are often hard and complex to implement in organizations, because they require substantial changes in the organizational structure of tasks and responsibilities.

The realization of such organizational integration by enterprise systems requires integration at different levels. This can be done at the interface of organization and information technology. For each integration level, the presented MS-Visio templates and models may be of use, as shown in Table 4.4.

For model integration a *meta-language* is required. A meta-language enables a representation by a set of symbols and lines that incorporates all the submodels and even manages the consistency between the models. These representations should be representations of the basic a priori concepts of the organization, and the meanings of these representations should be shared among the people modeling the reality. The one-to-one link between a priori and representation object is an analytic effort, and the way these a prioris can be used and related to form, e.g. a business model, is a synthetic effort. Figure 4.9 gives a list of key a prioris and the representation objects commonly used. Remember, though, that different methods and techniques of modeling may use different objects.

To ease and speed up the modeling efforts, substantial effort is being made to develop so-called *reference models*. Reference models may consist

Table 4.4 Integration perspectives and methods

Integration level	Perspective	Useful models	Integration method
Organization	Where; organizational	Organization charts	Restructuring and reorganization; removing redundant jobs and creating liaisons where needed
Business process	How and where; flowchart and (cross-functional) workflow	Cross-functional workflow and work schedules	Process reference models and process standards
Organizational knowledge	Why and when	Brainstorming and knowledge models; knowledge repositories	Best practices (selected best insights) and ontologies (standards of terminology and integration of partial insights in a larger knowledge network)
Applications	Who	For example, decision support applications; planning systems; agenda systems; communication tools; email; video-conferencing; electronic meeting systems	Inter-operability of applications; integration of systems in larger enterprise packages
Data	What	Data models	Data standards and terminology (semantic) standards
IT infrastructure	IT	Communication technology; services; security	IT standards; IT security policies; IT corporate infrastructure

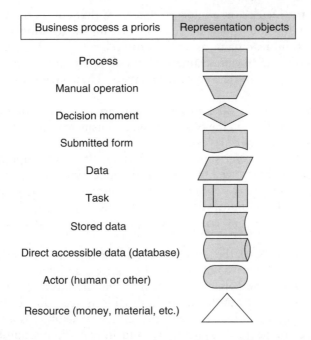

Figure 4.9 Business process a prioris and example representations.

of complete models for specific tasks and processes for specific industries. Sometimes (de facto) laws, like the famous Sarbanes–Oxley Act for administrative systems, specify specific procedures for administrative processes, and non-compliance to these reference models may result in legal issues. Also, the total quality management movement has created process models named "best practices" that correspond to specific quality standards (like the ISO 9000 standards). Sometimes reference models are the outcome of empirical research that detected the best way of working in certain industries (this is, for example, often the case with so-called evidence-based protocols in the health industry). This last type of reference models is not synthetic a priori but a posteriori (see also Becker *et al.* 2007a and 2007b).

It goes beyond the scope of this introductory book to further discuss the subjects of meta-languages and meta-modeling, so please refer to the work of Scheer (1998), who has developed an integrated modeling framework named ARIS, and Green and Rosemann (2000), who have developed criteria for comparing the quality of models.

An interesting development, though, from the perspective of model integration, is the developmental insights in *enterprise architectures*, which we explain here by one of its modeling languages, named *ArchiMate*. The ArchiMate language has been developed for modeling enterprise architectures. From its philosophy, it does not model one specific architectural

domain, but it focuses on a wider architecture that covers the whole organization. ArchiMate thus enables the possibility to model the global
structure within a domain, as well as the relationships between different
domains. In the ArchiMate framework the different architectural domains
are mapped onto three different design layers. These layers are:

1   The *business* layer offer products and services to external customers,
    which are realized in the organization by business processes (performed
    by business actors or roles).
2   The *application* layer supports the business layer with application ser-
    vices which are realized by (software) application components.
3   The *technology* layer offers infrastructural services (e.g. processing,
    storage, and communication services) needed to run applications, real-
    ized by computer and communication devices and system software.

Looking at Figure 4.10, the left-hand side of the grid gives the passive structure aspect, which consists of information objects and data structures. The
middle part gives the behavioral aspect of the architecture, i.e. it defines
the actions that transform the information objects according to the requirements. The right-hand side gives the active structure aspect, i.e. the
organized set of people, applications, and information technologies that
realize the behavior needed. ArchiMate identifies the following domains in
an architecture as relevant combinations of its layers and aspects:

•   The *information* domain holds all information that is relevant to enter-
    prise architecture from a business perspective.
•   The *product* domain describes the products or services that are offered
    by an organization to its customers.
•   The *process* domain describes the business functions and their
    processes.
•   The *organization* domain describes the actors and the roles they have
    in the business processes.
•   The *data* domain describes what type of data can be automatically
    processed.
•   The *application* domain describes the software applications that enable
    the business functions and processes.
•   The *technical infrastructure* domain describes the technical hardware
    platforms and the communication they have with the supported applica-
    tions.

The *ArchiMate language* abstracts from domain-specific concepts, making
it possible to create an enterprise architecture model of heterogeneous
domains.

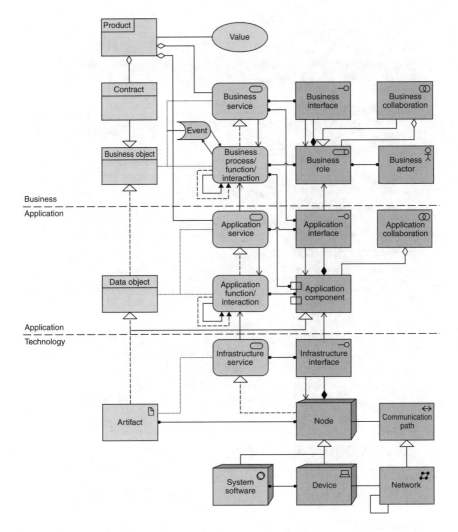

Figure 4.10 Three layers with concepts and relations of ArchiMate.

Source: Jonkers *et al.* (2004). Reprinted with permission from Springer Heidelburg.

With these layers and domain-specific descriptions, a set of main concepts has been made, which forms the basis of the ArchiMate language. A detailed overview of the concepts is given in the ArchiMate Quick Reference (www.telin.nl/index.cfm?language=nl&handle=52048&type=doc). Figure 4.10 gives the main concepts of the ArchiMate systems architecture language. Top-down it shows the business layer, the application layer, and the technology layer. For different stakeholders, different views can be identified that only show the relevant information per stakeholder.

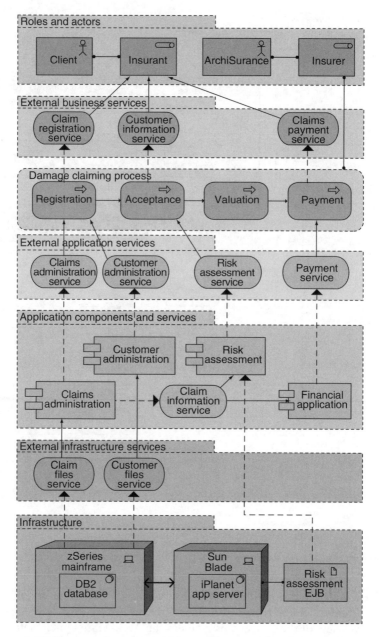

Figure 4.11 Service-oriented enterprise architecture of an insurance company.

Source: Jonkers *et al.* (2004). Reprinted with permission from Springer Heidelburg.

Figure 4.11 gives an example of a service-oriented architecture of an insurance company modeled with the ArchiMate framework. The example shows eight different layers which cover the three main layers: the business, application, and technology layers. On each level different components or roles are identified; for example, the client role, which is a client of the ArchiSurance company. The business services are in this example related to the specific business processes. The business processes are realized by the application services and components. The components are in turn realized by the IT infrastructure and IT components. The figure explicitly shows that all components in the enterprise and IT architecture are related to each other. This enables quick-impact analyses of changes and migrations in IT integration projects. The concepts in the ArchiMate view are chosen on such a generic level that processes and IT components are visible and linked to the front end of an organization: the customer and the products of the organization.

Reflective practice

In the previous chapter, I stated that modeling is important for making complex issues manageable. One may say that multi-perspective modeling, though, increases complexity and is thus opposed to the basic idea of modeling. This is not true, because, as Kant teaches us, the world can be seen from different perspectives, and in fact we should be able to work with multiple perspectives or we fail to cover phenomena sufficiently. Indeed, single-perspective modeling in many organizational contexts may even be worse than no modeling at all. Nevertheless, some division of work in complex modeling is needed, and Sowa and Zachman's classification of abstraction layers and our classification of integration levels (from organization to IT infrastructure) is useful, because it also refers to people with different types of expertise in an organization.

What does this imply for everyday life? Well, let's, for instance, model the who, what, when, what, why, and how aspects of learning while reading this book. Include in the models the processes and activities, organizational-responsible people/functions, databases they need, and possible software.

Another example. Take the case of the class reunion of Chapter 2. How does multi-perspective modeling help in organizing the reunion and its many activities? Use MS-Visio and select from the Business Process, Flowchart, Database, Network, and Organization categories to model the class reunion.

Finally, use the ArchiMate templates to design a service which enables reunion organizers to easily set up reunions via the Internet. What business services and processes, and what applications and infrastructures, should be developed?

Further reading

Elementary further reading

Kroenke, D. M. (2008) *Experiencing Management Information Systems*. Upper Saddle River, NJ: Pearson Prentice Hall, especially pp. 421–450.

On Kant's philosophy

Watkins, E. (2007) "Kant's philosophy of science," in E. N. Zalta (ed.) *The Stanford Encyclopedia of Philosophy* (Winter 2007 Edition), http://plato.stanford.edu/archives/win2007/entries/kant-science; accessed May, 2008.

On enterprise information systems

Davenport, T. (1998) "Putting the enterprise into the enterprise system," *Harvard Business Review*, July/August: 121–133.

On business process modeling and process integration

Green, P. and Rosemann, M. (2000) "Integrated process modeling: An ontological evaluation," *Information Systems*, 25(2): 73–87.
Scheer, A. (1998) *Aris: Business Process Frameworks*. Heidelberg, Germany: Springer.

On multi-perspective modeling

Jonkers, H., Lankhorst, M., Van Buuren, R., Hoppenbrouwers, S., Bonsangue, M., and Van der Torre, L. (2004) "Concepts for modelling enterprise architectures," *International Journal of Cooperative Information Systems*, 13(3): 257–287.
Kingston, J. and MacIntosh, A. (2000) "Knowledge management through multi-perspective modeling: Representing and distributing organizational memory," *Knowledge-Based Systems*, 13: 121–131.
Mingers, J. (2001) "Combining IS research methods: Towards a pluralist methodology," *Information Systems Research*, 12(3): 240–259.
Sowa, J. and Zachman, J. (1992) "Extending and formalizing the framework for information systems architecture," *IBM Systems Journal*, 31(3): 590–616.

On organizational modeling in general

Weick, K. E. (1979) *The Social Psychology of Organizing*, second edition. New York: Random House.

On organizational consequences of Kant's work

Courtney, J. (2001) "Decision making and knowledge management in inquiring organizations: Toward a new decision-making paradigm for DSS," *Decision Support Systems*, 31: 17–38.

5 The Hegelian view and information politics

Introduction to the philosophy of Hegel

Hegel[1]

Georg Wilhelm Friedrich Hegel was a German philosopher and, with Johann Gottlieb Fichte and Friedrich Schelling, one of the representatives of German idealism.

Hegel's work has a reputation for its difficulty and for the breadth of the topics it attempts to cover. Hegel introduced a dialectic system for understanding the history of philosophy and the world itself, often described as *a progression in which each successive movement emerges as a solution to the contradictions inherent in the preceding movement.* Churchman (1971) describes Hegel's dialectic as a three-step process of "Thesis, antithesis, synthesis," namely that a "thesis" (e.g. the French Revolution) causes the creation of its "antithesis" (e.g. the Reign of Terror that followed), which eventually results in a "synthesis" (e.g. the constitutional state of free citizens).[2] Churchman takes Hegel's view on thesis and antithesis as two different views about a phenomenon, based on different interests and *weltanschauungen* people may have. To find the truth in such cases is difficult, but most important for the progress of human insight. There are two ways of solving the resulting conflicts (i.e. realizing a synthesis). One way is to appoint a master who decides like a referee; the other is finding a joint resolution. An example here is a court case, in which the lawyer will selectively use the available data to find arguments in favor of his client. This may easily result in a biased view and even in a distorted view of reality. In contrast, the public prosecutor will try to show the errors and distortions the lawyer presents, and may also use selectively other data to demonstrate that the accused must be penalized. In some cases, the judge will not be requested to make a verdict when the two parties are able to settle the dispute (synthesis by resolution), but when this is hard to realize, the judge (or jury) will have to decide (i.e. synthesis by the master).

Consequences for information management

Despite the controversies regarding Hegel's intentions on dialectic logic, we take a lot of relevant insights from his epistemology, especially in the context of historical, political, or ethical information. Hegel's view that a historic trend (thesis) has its counter-trend (antithesis) is also relevant in the present. These trends have their protagonists using data about the same phenomena to find evidence for their arguments. People have a tendency to find some argument to reconcile the conflict, call it "whole," or "synthesis." For information management this implies that information is just part of the political struggle. An issue here is that people are often intentionally manipulated (or more politely stated, "convinced"), and that this is done by data bias and manipulation which is hard to detect. This is especially so with content on the Internet, because the Internet is a free platform for anyone to deliver his or her information and views to anyone in the world, and the size of the number of messages makes it difficult to know the quality and opinion status of each message.[3] In this context, information management should provide people with the tools to detect bias and create their own opinion via a critical analysis of data provided. This is quite different from the Lockean, Leibnizian, and Kantian models (see Figure 5.1).

For information management, the consequences can be summarized as:

1   Different sources may deliver conflicting representations depending on the world view and interests behind it, because in an open communicative environment (like the Internet) a representation of some historical event (thesis) will cause a representation of the same event by an opponent (antithesis).
2   The detection of these sources of bias is a key challenge in a world of information overload.
3   So we need systems that are able to triangulate (i.e. compare data by different sources, views, methods, and investigators) data and sources. There are different ways of triangulation, which will be explained later in this chapter.
4   When triangulating data, we become part of the debate again and not slaves of anonymous forces.

The key ideas of the Hegelian model are summarized in Figure 5.2.

Before we go further on triangulation later in the chapter, we will first describe how people can get access to the many different representations of historic phenomena.

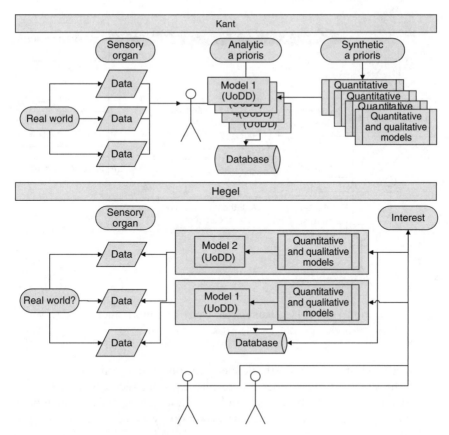

Figure 5.1 Comparison of Kant and Hegel.

Collecting data on the Internet

Internet information intermediation

The Internet has huge virtual piles of information.[4] This results in a substantial feeling of information overload or senselessness. Intermediating tools, like the Google search engine, can help people find what they need.

The aim of any search activity is, of course, to receive documents with sufficient recall and precision, i.e. existing documents that are not relevant need to be omitted, and what is gained should be sufficiently precise. To realize this, we need a good *query*, which can be created by the following:

1 Define what you need, and think before you "leap" (i.e. state your search sentence clearly).

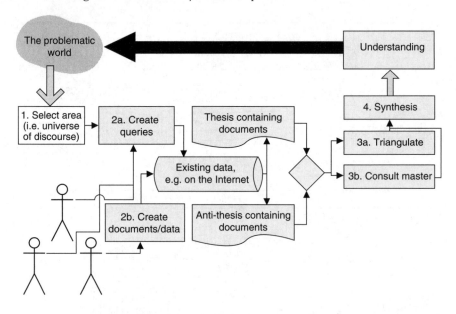

Figure 5.2 A model of the Hegelian epistemology and information management.

2   Specify your need and rethink specifications and alternatives.
3   If the specified query does not result in proper recall (i.e. all relevant documents should be found) and precision (i.e. irrelevant documents will not be presented), generalize your query or navigate from a reasonably interesting resource.
4   Additionally, one has to be selective with regard to the interpretation of the *results* gained from an Internet query. As a general rule one can state that the first twenty search results should be satisfactory; if not, you may need to rethink the query.

Technological improvements in information retrieval on the Internet are large and diverse, but are not able to solve user-oriented search problems alone. Lawrence and Giles (1999), for instance, report a recall (coverage with respect to estimated web size) of 16 percent and precision (percentage of valid links retrieved) of 14 percent for the best performing search engine (in 1999). These performances may have been worse up until now and in the future, because of the rapid growth of the Internet's content base. An information service, i.e. a value-adding intermediary between suppliers and users of Internet data, may reduce information overload by deciding on what a relevant delivery is for the information customer. Given the multi-actor nature of information services, its business models may be conceptualized as value nets (Stabell and Fjeldsted,

1998): some actors deliver or collect content (C), some deliver user features like software for viewing and interacting with content (U), while others may receive revenues (R). This is presented in the value-net model (which describes actors and their mutual relations in terms of their mutual value exchanges) of Figure 5.3, but it is often unclear what exactly a good service is in this context. Besides the previously mentioned technical information retrieval tools (search engines), the match between supplied content and customer needs may require some human intermediation as well. Human intermediation can consist of a handling of the meaning of messages to avoid semantic conflicts, or further interactions with the users concerning their needs, so-called pragmatic service, or the development of human interactions between suppliers and customers, so that they can realize any information exchange themselves in an informal way. In addition to content matching (technical, semantic, pragmatic, or social), an information service may act content-sensitive (instead of content-blind; MacKie-Mason *et al.*, 1996) through facilitating content verification. Figure 5.3 summarizes these services in the context of the Internet.

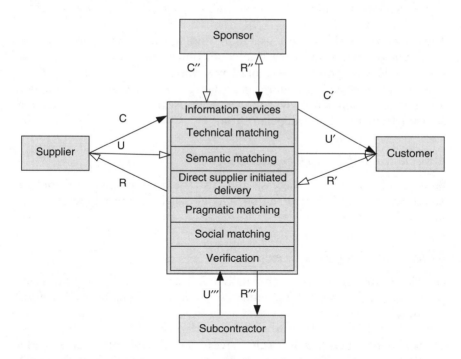

Figure 5.3 Information services and their value nets on the Internet.

Notes
The open arrow heads denote optional relations; figure based on Wijnhoven and Kraaijenbrink (2008).

Technical intermediation: Search engines

Search engines automatically index files submitted to an Internet location. A major search engine is www.google.com (which will be discussed later), but alternatives exist like www.alltheweb.com, www.altavista.com, www.yahoo.com, search.msn.com, and www.ask.com.

All these alternatives at the time of writing (April, 2008) lack sufficient functionality to beat Google, though www.ask.com is rather interesting because of its options to query in *natural language. Meta search engines* aim at improving precision and recall using results of multiple search engines. Several meta search engines have been developed in the past, such as www.ixquick.com, www.vivisimo.com, www.kartoo.com, and www.dogpile.com. Also *specialized search engines* are currently offered to improve recall and precision in specific areas, such as:

- searching on topics (e.g. sports or social sciences);
- searching on region (e.g. limited to Dutch or French resources);
- searching on medium (e.g. music files or jpeg).

The following websites are useful in finding such specialized engines: www. google.com/dirhp, www.beaucoup.com, www.allsearchengines.com, www.pandia.com/powersearch, and www.searchengineguide.com.

The following sites give more up-to-date *information on search engines*: searchenginewatch.com, www.infopeople.org/search, and www.bruceclay.com/searchenginerelationshipchart.htm.

A special case of a search engine: Google

Because of its market success, and also because of its excellence in functionality, recall, and precision, Google needs a special treatment in this book.

Basics of the Google search engine

Google is able to process maximally 32 search terms at a time using Boolean logic (i.e. "and," "or," and "not" statements) (January 23, 2005).[5] Examples:

1 Searching "Bert" and "Ernie" gives you all available sources about Bert and Ernie. You may use the Boolean operator OR for this as well.
2 Searching by "Bert" + "Ernie" gives you all available sources that combine the Bert and Ernie information.
3 Searching by "Bert and Ernie" delivers only exact matches.
4 You may reduce the chance of irrelevant hits by the minus operator. For instance, "Bert" – "Ernie" only gives sources about Bert, but not for Ernie.

5   Google also offers the opportunity to search on a specific date, though using the date in the option "with exact combination of words" is probably more efficient.

Special functionalities of Google

1   Search a site by site:sitename; e.g. site:Amsterdam.nl.
2   Search by countries; e.g. site:.nl.
3   Retrieving lost websites. This is feasible via the cache or html options that are presented in search results. This option also often allows you to search pages that require logins (but did not require logins before).
4   Search on document types like pdf via filetype:pdf, ps, doc, xls, ppt, rtf. Such a search may reveal very interesting resources, like budget information (by searching on xls extensions).
5   Dictionaries and descriptions of phenomena can be found via the "define: . . ." statement in Google.
6   Synonyms can be handled by putting a tilde (~) before the search term. This enables, for example, the search for "helicopter" and "chopper" at the same time.
7   The link option enables you to find sites that are linked to an existing site so that possible other sources with comparable information can be found. The is done by link:www.amsterdam.nl and link:amsterdam.nl; use both options because of the possible inconsistencies in the links.

Google is *continuously evolving*, and many interesting options are still in beta or experimental stages. These can be found at labs.google.com. Two interesting options available on Google Labs in May 2007 are:

•   Labs.google.com/personalized, which enables you to create a personal profile to help Google focus on specific and more relevant search results to suit you.
•   Labs.google.com/sets enables you to find complete sets of phenomena belonging to a few key terms you entered. For example, Clinton, Roosevelt, and Bush gives you a list of the US presidents since 1776, but also some related people like Nixon's secretary of state Henry Kissinger.

Semantic intermediation: Internet guides and the deep web

An Internet guide indexes and structures content by human editors. This means that the content and structure of the guide is based on a *human meaning of relevance*. Although this may be a strong advantage over technical intermediation, it results in:

- structures which are nearly never complete and unsatisfactory from the perspective of users; and
- the structure will be more selective than the structure that is automatically generated by a search engine.

Creating search guides is mostly the effort of *volunteers,* and its value raises when the expertise is more specific and specialized. For more general information, a search engine probably will do better.

A *few interesting internet guides* are:

- directory.yahoo.com: this guide has a commercial flavor;
- www.about.com: better to use the categories instead of the search field on this site; an interesting one is politicalhumor.about.com;
- directory.google.com;
- www.ipl.org: a good guide for academic search efforts;
- international.loc.gov/www.loc.gov: these are high-quality guides from the Library of Congress;
- www.rdn.ac.uk: collects websites on academic disciplines.

Probably only 1 percent of the total Internet can be searched by public sources like Google. This means that 99 percent of the Internet is invisible or that one can only see the front page of the site but not the data needed. This publicly unreachable or not-indexed data is called the *deep web.* There are several tricks to still get access (see our discussion on Google). Some guides have specialized advice in getting access to the deep web, such as:

- infomine.ucr.edu: particularly suitable for academic information sources;
- www.invisible-web.net;
- www.completeplanet.com: a bit more commercial than the previous one;
- www.beaucoup.com: also quite commercial.

A specific problem with search engines is the handling of the many natural languages of the world. You may need translation software to search non-English or mother tongue languages. Alternatives for this are:

- www.systranet.com;
- www.google.com/language_tools;

Pragmatic intermediation: Intermediated search

A number of *expert services* are available via the Internet which can help people to find the right kind of information, such as:

- www.loc.gov/rr/askalib: a free service from the US Library of Congress;
- www.ipl.org/div/askus;

- www.ask-a-librarian.org.uk;
- www.nls.uk/info/readingrooms/askalibrarian.html: handles a broader range of issues than the previous version;
- www.allexperts.com;
- www.profnet.com;
- www.madsci.org/submit.html: for questions aimed at scientists.

Supplier-oriented delivery: RSS and alerts

Alert services deliver content to customers when this fits an agreement with them. Some tools for this are:

- www.googlealert.com: sends you emails if something new is available on the Internet on a specific topic;
- www.aignes.com: delivers the tool WebSite-Watcher, which has a better recall and precision than Google alert, though it is not free after a trial period.

RSS (really simple syndication) gives specified and filtered newsletters without the risk of receiving spam, because it does not need your email address. Instead, the website you want to check has to offer an RSS facility, and you need to install an RSS reader. RSS can also be usefully combined for checking weblogs. Some RSS tools are www.newsgator.com (high quality, although not for free) and www.feeddemon.com. Some RSS tools do not need you to install a RSS reader, like www.bloglines.com, www.google.com/reader, and www.bloogz.com.

RSS feeds can be found by, for example, www.newisfree.com/sources/bycat and www.rootblog.com, and also via Google by site address and an rss, rdf, or xml extension, e.g. site:nytimes rss.

Social intermediation: Social software and Internet communities

There are several ways of exchanging information between people, without fully codifying the content. The oldest is *Usenet,* which offers discussion facilities, chat, and unfortunately also some illegal practices. Interestingly, Usenet's resources contain documentations of discussions since 1981. Also, Google has incorporated many of these discussions options via groups.google.com. *Email lists* can be very useful for staying ahead of a certain topic or influencing opinions on a topic. There are a number of lists such as groups.yahoo.com, www.lsoft.com/lists/listref.html, lists.topica.com, and www.webscoutlists.com. *Chat services* enable all kinds of informal interactions between people. The problem with chat services is that sometimes illegal practices are conducted over it. Therefore, it may be wise to use a nickname instead of your real name. If you want to know who the person you are chatting with is, you can use the option/whois nickname. Some chat services are: www.mirc.com, people.icq.com, messenger.msn.com, members.yahoo.com, www.aim.com, and www.ceruleanstudios.com.

Some Internet tools aim to group people around topics, so-called *communities,* and match them in networks, such as www.orkut.com, www. friendster.com, www.linkedin.com, and www.facebook.com.

Handling information conflicts: Information triangulation

The idea of information triangulation

In science, a good researcher triangulates (uses multiple methods, data sources, and researches) to enhance the validity of his or her findings. It limits personal and methodological biases. In other words, by triangulating, the researcher makes his or her findings more trustworthy. Triangulating online news would thus be a good way to improve the perceived trustworthiness. Denzin (1970) was the first to propose triangulation as a research strategy. He outlines four types of triangulation, namely data triangulation, investigator triangulation, theory triangulation, and methodological triangulation. These types of triangulation are discussed in this section.

Data triangulation

Data triangulation is the affirmative use of different data sources. These can be different types of material like books, photos, films, and sound or the same material in different places in time and space. Triangulation of this kind can be done in two ways:

1   One way is to give the information searcher evidence through alternative media, such as photos, movies, data, and text, so that the evidence can be compared and checked on consistencies.
2   The other way consists of giving the information searcher opportunities to track and trace evidence through space and time, so that original sources can be checked.

A lot of websites are not what they really are, and a lot of information on the Internet is definitely misleading and incorrect. Suspicion is therefore a good and necessary attitude. Three possibilities exist to quickly check, triangulate, and verify websites and their information:

1   Check the owner of the website. If this is not clear, do not trust the site. Ownership of websites can be checked by the whois-database, which is a public registry of domain site owners accessible via www.allwhois. com, www.whoisfinder.com, and http://hexillion.com/co.

2　Checking who else or what other websites link to the site accessed. This may give a second opinion about the original site. You may use the following for this: Google's link option, www.hotbot.com, and www.linkpopularity.com.

3　Traceroutes finding and reverse DNS scanning. Via traceroutes you can find the specific geographic location of the site, and with reverse DNS you can find other websites of the same website owner. Traceroutes can be detected by www.traceroute.com and www.visualroute.com (not for free); reverse DNS can be scanned by www.dnsstuff.com.

Investigator triangulation

Investigator triangulation brings other investigators into the research. This can, for example, be done by working in a team, independently examining a part of the data and checking the prior interpretations, or letting an auditor regularly check the process. Investigator triangulation on online news can be realized by including different journalists/correspondents (investigators). This can be done by providing search engines with articles from different investigators.

Investigator triangulation on the Internet may involve a few steps:

1　First it involves the specification of a certain topic. It should be clear what the scope of the topic is.

2　Next, a few sources should be identified, which are queried along the topic. These sources can be organizations (like press agencies) or individuals (like reporters). The former mostly have publication websites; the latter mostly have blogs.

3　A content analysis can be done to see the differences. The differences can exist in the different terms used (this can be done by a word count in MS-Word), different conclusions (like predictions for the future, normative claims in terms of good and bad, empirical statements if something did happen or not), different data (differences in evidence given), and the size of the documents (as a criterion for importance).

Theory triangulation

Theory triangulation (also called theoretical triangulation) involves using multiple perspectives or theories to interpret a single set of data. For example, when there is an armed conflict somewhere in the world, one can look at it from an economic perspective (invasion to secure oil reserves) or from a human perspective (invasion to stop inhuman actions of a state). Theory triangulation as an information management activity on the Internet can be done by the following process:

1   Define the topic scope.
2   Select representative key terms and queries on the topic and use these in your search engine.
3   Define the perspective you want for theory triangulation. This could be economic, human, cultural, political, or technical. Key economic terms are, for instance, income, profit, and economic growth. Human terms are, for instance, aid, birth, death, population, happiness, and sadness. Cultural terms are, for instance, music, literature, dance, and art. Political terms are, for instance, power, election, government, state, and army. Technical terms are, for instance, speed, efficiency, invention, and science.
4   Depending on the topic, you may want to select several of these key terms and combine them with the results to dig further. Each term may need a different selection of document. Find the documents which are not overlapping (exclusive) and check the abstracts and key issues.

Methodological triangulation

Methodological triangulation (also called method triangulation) refers to the use of different methods to examine a phenomenon. This can be done by within-method triangulation (using varieties of the same method) and between-methods triangulation (using a combination of different methods).

Research methodologists have discussed widely the different types of evidence that can be collected and the different conclusions that can be drawn on the basis of this. These methodologies may be:

1   *Empirical.* This focuses on the collection of data of measurements, which as a next step can be put in databases and be in some way quantitatively analyzed. Census offices and research institutions can often be successfully queried for this purpose.
2   *Interpretive.* This focuses on what people think and have in their mind, which can be found by personal interviews and in-depth interviews. These data are mostly analyzed in a qualitative way. These data can often be found in newspapers, especially background articles.
3   *Historical.* This involves finding evidence to explain people's so-called "genuine because" motives, i.e. not what they say why they do certain things but by finding motivations they find from a joint history, which is a foundation for shared beliefs and intentions. These data are often provided by historians and political scientists.
4   *Critical.* This focuses on finding opinions and ideas for change. These can be collected by document research (e.g. political party programs and public statements of politicians and chief executives).

Any document found on the Internet on a certain topic can be analyzed for the presence or absence of these four data modes. One can also triangulate by using different key words with similar meanings in a query.

Example: Causes of global warming

Going to www.google.com, we entered "earth warming" and the first hit gained on February 6, 2008 was http://weather.about.com/od/ climatechange/i/collingearth.html. This page discusses the pro and contra arguments of the "human causes of global warming" hypothesis. The editor, Rachelle Oblack, shows both arguments, with the general conclusion being that the impact of human action is undeniable. One could consider that maybe she is biased by Al Gore's opinion-making machinery and the political network around him, which is undeniable large and influential, so it is wise to check her background and the background of the site she is running.

The site is part of the "about.com" pages, which are co-write protected and owned by "The New York Times Company." This company has a reputation for high-quality journalism and ambitions to have an independent opinion in the political arena. Rachelle Oblack, according to the website, "is a multi-award winning K-12 science teacher and writer. Aa a true science lover, Mrs Oblack was among the top 197 Educator Astronaut applicants in the country. She was subsequently invited to join the Network of Educator Astronaut Teachers (NEAT). She has written for various sources including the Newshour Extra with Jim Lehrer Lessons."

The following is again a demonstration of assumed objectivity and independence. The weather.about.com site also links through to the United Nations platforms on weather and earth warming, but the site is sponsored by www.neshama.info and "Free book on prophecy," two very clearly Christian movements. *Data triangulation* in this case may seem easy, as the site clearly states the owner and people responsible for its messages. *Investigator triangulation* is partially done by linking to alternative sources, although it is not clear why *these* have been selected. *Theory triangulation* discovers the link between this site and Christian movements, but it is unclear if this link has been made intentional by the site owner or made by this movement with or without acknowledgment from the site owner. The site itself, though, links explicitly to a United Nations source, which may suggest an independent and multi-perspective view. *Methodological triangulation* is realized through the provision of textual data and visual presentations of information. It may also be achieved by alternative key words in the query. Very common words denoting what we actually are interested in (human or non-human causes for global warming) are "Kyoto discussion," "global warming," "climate change," and "an inconvenient truth."

We may conclude also that the about.com view may have some bias. So let's see if we can find alternative viewpoints (theoretical triangulation), maybe more radical or maybe a counter-view. It took to searching 24 documents before one site was found with a critical view on the "human causes of earth warming" hypothesis. This is the site: http://medienkritik. typepad.com/blog/2007/02/a_sane_voice_ab.html (accessed January 25, 2008). Who are these people? Well, a site named "medien kritik" with the subtitle of "politically incorrect observations on reporting in the German media." The site seems to be committed to Karl Popper's critical rational- ism, which sees open discussion and criticism as the basis for scientific and social progress. The site is run by David Kaspar and Ray Drake. Searching their site, I found the following section about their mission statement:

> Davids Medienkritik is a collection of critical postings written by those who run this blog (David and Ray) on the German media. Occasionally we also publish political postings that have no connection to any par- ticular media organization, particularly if the topic is current and plays an important role in public discussion.
>
> Our criticism is from a "politically incorrect" point of view—our position is pro-American, pro-Israeli and pro-capitalist. As a rule we compose our postings in English because we want to inform our English-speaking audience as to the situation in the German media and where possible, also fill them in on German politics.
>
> We welcome comments as an addition, but the main purpose of our blog is the publication of our postings along the lines of the above-described blog philosophy. Davids Medienkritik was not cre- ated to serve primarily as a discussion forum or chat room.

So that is clear. Let's see if anyone has real arguments against the "earth warming" proposition.

It took some time but document 55 looks different: www.answerbag. com/q_view/339769 (accessed January 25, 2008). A question on this site is:

> It seems the sun is the cause of the earth's warming (go figure): www.webcommentary.com/climate/climate.php. Do you think Al Gore and Michael Moore will accept the science or will they keep up the con in the interest of making $$$?

Okay, so who is Answerbag?

> Answerbag is a community of people helping others. Have a question? Ask it here! Know something? (Everyone knows something!) Help someone out! We're here to help you connect with others and to find and share knowledge about topics ranging from celebrity trivia and home cleaning tips to Russian name origins and particle physics. Any topic you can dream of, you can ask it here!

Whom do you trust? Your mother may have told you that you can't trust everything you read on the Internet, and she's right. As you browse the 'net, you find sites that you think are accurate, but whom can you really trust? Can you trust a message board posting? A hobby or fan site that was last updated in 1996? A commerce site that's trying to sell you something? It's difficult to know who really knows what they are talking about. It's worse than politics.

Information democracy Answerbag brings trust to information on the web. Every bit of info on this site can be voted on, so trustworthy answers are promoted and the chaff is weeded out. People just like you tell if they think an answer was useful, and if most people agree, you'll see that answer is "trusted." This lets you know that it isn't just some loony like my Uncle Herb giving you his answer—it's a group of people who have come together to agree on an answer.

The Internet has brought about the first time in history when people around the globe have had the ability to freely share and compare their knowledge and expertise. Gone are the political and geographic boundaries that once restricted information flow.

Conclusion: a commercial site aiming at a new way of publishing, and of course for generating money. They have no specific ideology, except that they have to become popular and thus earn money by facilitating the demand and supply of information. They do this well aware of Internet-content politics, though, as they often have no way for triangulation, they leave Internet information politics to the reader and information supplier.

Wikipedia as a social Internet mediator

After all this checking and triangulating, one may ask if it is possible to generate something like truth via the Internet. To some extent people can collectively do much better, though, by organizing and moderating the Internet. A quite good example here is Wikipedia.org. For instance, check the Wikipedia.org page on "global warming" and you will find text that meets triangulation criteria to a great extent. Data triangulation is facilitated in offering many diverse types of data (pictures, texts, data, video, etc.). Investigator triangulation is more or less directly realized via the open nature of Wikipedia, which allows anyone with insights to deliver a contribution. The editorial team, though, checks the quality, so that clearly inconsistent, incorrect, or non-contributing submissions are avoided. Theoretical triangulation is realized by the open nature of Wikipedia and the explicit collection of different views on global warming. In contrast to the Internet, therefore, it is easy to find discussions of non-humanly caused global warming. Finally, methodological triangulation is enabled via the different data and approaches that are discussed at that page. The reader is highly recommended to check the Wikipedia global warming page on http://en.wikipedia.org/wiki/Global_warming and to check Wikipedia's procedures and policies on http://en.wikipedia.org/wiki/Wikipedia:About. A few of their key activities regarding social intermediation are given below (quoted from their own homepage) (accessed February 5, 2008).

Wikipedia is written collaboratively by volunteers from all around the world. Since its creation in 2001, Wikipedia has grown rapidly into one of the largest reference Web sites. There are more than 75,000 active contributors working on some 9,000,000 articles in more than 250 languages. As of today, there are 2,241,222 articles in English; every day hundreds of thousands of visitors from around the world make tens of thousands of edits and create thousands of new articles to enhance the knowledge held by the Wikipedia encyclopedia. (See also: Wikipedia:Statistics.)

Visitors do not need specialized qualifications to contribute, since their primary role is to write articles that cover existing knowledge; this means that people of all ages and cultural and social backgrounds can write Wikipedia articles. With rare exceptions, articles can be edited by anyone with access to the Internet, simply by clicking the "edit this page" link. Anyone is welcome to add information, cross-references or citations, as long as they do so within Wikipedia's editing policies and to an appropriate standard. For example, if you add information to an article, be sure to include your references, as unreferenced facts are subject to removal.

As a *wiki,* articles are never complete. They are continually edited and improved over time, and in general this results in an upward trend of quality, and a growing consensus over a fair and balanced representation of information. Because Wikipedia is an ongoing work to which, in principle, anybody can contribute, it differs from a paper-based reference source in important ways. In particular, older articles tend to be more comprehensive and balanced, while newer articles more frequently contain significant misinformation, unencyclopedic content, or vandalism. Users need to be aware of this to obtain valid information and avoid misinformation that has been recently added and not yet removed (see Researching with Wikipedia for more details). However, unlike a paper reference source, Wikipedia is continually updated, with the creation or updating of articles on topical events within seconds, minutes or hours, rather than months or years for printed encyclopedias. [. . .]

The ideal Wikipedia article is balanced, neutral and encyclopedic, containing comprehensive notable, verifiable knowledge. An increasing number of articles reach this standard over time, and many already have. The best articles are called Featured Articles (and display a small star in the upper right corner of the article), and the second best tier of articles are designated Good Articles. However, this is a process and can take months or years to be achieved, as each user adds their contribution in turn. Some articles contain statements and claims which have not yet been fully cited. Others will later have entire new sections added. Some information will be considered by later contributors to be insufficiently founded, and may be removed or expounded.

While the overall trend is generally upward, it is important to use Wikipedia carefully if it is intended to be used as a research source, since individual articles will, by their nature, vary in standard and maturity. There are guidelines and information pages designed to help users and researchers do this effectively, and an article that summarizes third-party studies and assessments of the reliability of Wikipedia.

There is no need to worry about accidentally damaging Wikipedia when adding or improving information, as other editors are always around to advise or correct obvious errors, and Wikipedia's software, known as *MediaWiki*, is carefully designed to allow easy reversal of editorial mistakes.

Wikipedia is a registered trademark of the nonprofit Wikimedia Foundation, which has created an entire family of free-content projects. At a project level the Foundation also coordinates the global policies, practices and facilities of Wikipedia in all languages and its sister projects, provides legal and intellectual property input as required, and is formally responsible for the development of the open source Wikipedia software (*Mediawiki*) as requirements change. In line with its goal of producing reference material free to all people, the Foundation also operates a *Metawiki* where matters impinging upon all projects, global discussions can take place, and global policies can be formally documented and developed, and an incubator for proposed new projects and new languages, to facilitate their launch and early stage development. As of August 2007 there are around 100 new reference projects in various stages of development initiated by members of the Wikipedia and related communities. All of the text in Wikipedia, and most of the images and other content, is covered by the GNU Free Documentation License (GFDL). Contributions remain the property of their creators, while the GFDL license ensures the content is freely distributable and reproducible.

Several mechanisms are in place to help Wikipedia members carry out the important work of crafting a high-quality resource while maintaining civility. Editors are able to watch pages and techies can write editing programs to keep track of or rectify bad edits. Over 1,000 administrators with special powers ensure that behavior conforms to Wikipedia guidelines and policies. When a few situations are still unresolved after all other consensus remedies have failed, a judicial committee steps in and decides to withdraw or restrict editing privileges or to take other corrective measures.

Studies suggest that Wikipedia is broadly as reliable as *Encyclopedia Britannica,* with similar error rates on established articles for both major and minor omissions and errors. There is a tentative consensus, backed by a gradual increase in academic citation as a source, that it provides a good starting point for research, and that articles in general have proven to be reasonably sound. That said, articles and subject areas sometimes suffer from significant omissions, and while misinformation and vandalism are usually corrected quickly, this does not always happen. Therefore, a common conclusion is that it is a valuable resource and provides a good reference point on its subjects.

The *MediaWiki* software which runs Wikipedia retains a history of all edits and changes, thus information added to Wikipedia never "vanishes," and is never "lost" or deleted. Discussion pages are an important resource on contentious topics. There, serious researchers can often find a wide range of vigorously or thoughtfully advocated viewpoints not present in the consensus article. Like any source, information should be checked. A 2005 editorial by a BBC technology writer comments that these debates are probably symptomatic of new cultural learnings which are happening across all sources of information (including search engines and the media), namely "a better sense of how to evaluate information sources."

On truth in organizations

We now may be interested in thinking about whether the Internet in a moderated form, like Wikipedia, has sufficient abilities to realize truth. Well, here, we have to disappoint the reader, as truth is a very complex contextual term, and according to philosopher of science Karl Popper (1959) not reachable, and in fact we do not need it always fully. The progress of science is more served by criticism of what we think we know than being happy about what we have achieved, because the last attitude encourages dogmatism and totalitarian thinking in terms of so-called absolute truths. Particularly in organizational managerial contexts, so-called objective facts and figures are hard to find and in many situations not relevant. The reason is that management decisions are dependent on the following parameters (Hofstede, 1981):

1   The possibility to know the effects of management interventions. In the chapter on Leibniz, we assumed that managers are able to model their reality so that they can know the possible impact of what they do. The reality is that, in many management conditions, the *consequences may be unknown* because people can behave differently than expected and many environmental conditions change without any opportunity of management to influence this.

2   If actions of managers can be predicted, management actions can become pure *routine and automated* or, when the management conditions do not repeat themselves frequently, experts can make proper decisions. The last case is often when we hope that organizational consultants can help an organization solve its problems, because of the knowledge such a consultant is expected to have.

3   When effects of management interventions are not known (so no clear model of reality), decisions will have to be based on *intuition* or *trial and error* (when the activities and situations are repetitive). In trial and error conditions, databases may become very useful in supporting the detection of the best actions.

4   Information systems become especially important when it is feasible to measure output, a key part of management accounting. Unfortunately, objective output measurement is not always possible, and we will often have to make do with so-called *surrogate measures*. When acceptable surrogate measures can be found, and the effects of the intervention are known, information systems can be extremely useful in guiding management decisions. This is often realized and aimed at by management information and executive information systems. Unfortunately, satisfactory surrogate measures cannot easily be found, and therefore decisions will have to be frequently based on judgment. To illustrate the difficulties of using data for management decisions, consider financial reporting. Financial reports are important for investors to take decisions regarding selling or buying stocks on a stock exchange. These data therefore have to be correct and checked by independent accountants, who may adjust the incorrect bookkeeping practices of companies, or not agree with the report. Berenson (2003) describes the tendency of CEOs in the USA to disguise financial troubles and present the firm better, thereby raising the value of the stocks. This is mainly in the interests of the firm to attract additional funds and, especially, for the CEOs themselves, who often are partially or sometimes even largely paid by stock options. One of the typical bookkeeping tricks here is to book expenses (like salaries) as increased assets and to book the sales of assets (like patents and parts of the company) as regular business incomes. Although these practices give an overly optimistic picture of a company's financial situation, CEOs sometimes force their accountants to accept this practice, so that they can cash their options just before the company runs into financial trouble (Berenson, 2003). The CEOs can do this, because the accountants are paid by them and thus are not as independent as they are assumed to be. The Stock Exchange Committee (SEC), which supervises the quality of the financial reports, unfortunately is insufficiently equipped to check these reports. Berenson mentions that insufficient

budgets and people enabled the SEC only to check 2,280 of the 14,000 reports in 2001. This means that the information intermediary (the publisher of the reports and the Stock Exchange) is quite ineffective on its information market.

5   One important reason why output measurement is so difficult is the *ambiguity of objectives*. When this ambiguity cannot be solved, decision making is mainly a political affair. Nevertheless, political decision making needs legitimation, and informing is one of the main ways to achieve this. When informing is used for legitimation (often by the Internet, not only for politicians but also for companies who want to legitimate themselves), we cannot easily expect that this information is useful for understanding organizational processes or decision making. What it provides is understanding of what some people want and how they want to get others to support their objectives.

A summary of these insights on organizational truth gives Figure 5.4.

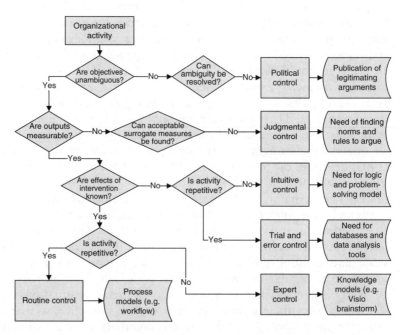

Figure 5.4 Types of organizational control and the role of information.

Source: Hofstede (1981). Adapted.

Reflective practice

Given the political nature of much (Internet) information, triangulation is a key mechanism to maintain some control over our understanding of the world as an information consumer. For this purpose triangulation needs to be a basic skill and tool. This chapter has provided several criteria and instruments for this, but can you make it a systematic personal skill? To be able to develop such abilities, four assignments are given below:

1   Define requirements for an Internet news triangulator. Evaluate what the triangulator has to offer, and what is available from Google and other tools. Try to realize the triangulator and test it on political issues or information on people available on the Internet. Search also at Google labs, www.lifehacker.com, and www.wiki.org for what useful triangulation tools are available.
2   Select a topic on which you have special expertise, search Wikipedia about it, and make a contribution as an author.
3   Write a manual for Google and on triangulation activities with your virtual learning group.
4   Find other tools besides Google for Internet search and triangulation and try to evaluate these tools on a set of criteria.
5   Develop a triangulation method for systematically discussing management reports.

Further reading

Elementary further reading

Kroenke, D. (2008) *Experiencing Management Information Systems*. Upper Saddle River, NJ: Pearson Prentice Hall, especially pp. 114–153 and 395–420.

Redding, P. (2006) "Georg Wilhelm Friedrich Hegel," in E. N. Zalta (ed.) *The Stanford Encyclopedia of Philosophy* (Fall 2006 Edition), http://plato.stanford.edu/archives/fall2006/entries/hegel; accessed May, 2008.

On triangulation and truth

Berenson, A. (2003) *The Number: How the Drive for Quarterly Earnings Corrupted Wall Street and Corporate America*. New York: Random House.

Denzin, N. (1970) *The Research Act: A Theoretical Introduction into Sociological Methods*. Chicago: Aldin.

Hofstede, G. (1981) "Management control of public and not-for-profit activities," *Accounting, Organizations and Society,* 6(3): 193–211.

On information on the Internet and search engines

Lawrence, S. and Giles, C. (1999) "Accessibility of information on the web," *Nature,* 400: 107–109.

MacKie-Mason, J., Shenker, S., and Varian, H. (1996) "Service architecture and content provision: The network provider as editor," *Telecommunications Policy,* 20(3): 203–218.

Wijnhoven, F. and Kraaijenbrink, J. (2008) "Product-oriented design theory for digital information services: A literature review," *Internet Research,* 18(1): 93–120.

6 Information management in organizations

From philosophy to organizational reality

The previous chapters have explained the nature of information from a philosophical approach, and in each chapter conclusions were drawn regarding handling information by modern IT means (databases, spreadsheets, search engines, social software, and organizational modeling tools). As stated in Chapter 1, the epistemologies of Locke, Leibniz, Kant, and Hegel focus mainly on the individual's veracity. Information management, though, is a social and institutionalized process, because the creation of an individual's understanding of the world is a collaborative effort and happens in a more or less organized context. This organizational context is able to give a group of information-searching persons resources (e.g. access to experts, libraries, and the Internet, and time and money to search) with a synergetic value over the resources that could be the sum of those of the individuals (Barnard, 1938). These *synergistic resources* consist of the opportunities to specialize in certain domains and specialize between information expertise and information technological expertise. Given an organization's strategic objectives, an organization may recognize the importance of developing large databases, to buy and modify large software systems for data processing, and develop IT infrastructures for optimized security and support to its IT users. The combination of IT resources and data can become a strategic capability for an organization, i.e. a capability by which the organization can become significantly better than other organizations. These aspects, organizational strategy, information systems, and IT capabilities, will be examined in the following sections. The question this chapter wants to answer is how organizational resources can be beneficial to achieving the goals and objectives the respective philosophers pursued.

For each of the previously mentioned philosophers, Courtney (2001) has defined organizational resources to meet their objectives. Regarding the *Lockean perspective* he states:

> A community of Lockean inquirers learns by observing the world, sharing observations, and creating a consensus about what has been observed.

Organizational knowledge is created through observation, interpretation, communication, and the development of shared meaning. The organization's culture or subculture (a Lockean community) must be supportive of this type of environment. That is, organizational members must feel free to observe and express opinions. Moreover, they must have a common language and mindset, which permits effective communication. The decision style is clearly group-oriented and open. Input is sought from a variety of sources, communication is encouraged, and consensus is sought. [...] Organizational knowledge is socially constructed through observation and discussion.

(Courtney, 2001: 26)

The primary organizational resources for these Lockean knowledge creation processes are data repositories, such as data warehouses (which combine several databases) for storing observations, data mining for analyzing these observations, and groupware tools, such as electronic meeting software, for facilitating the communication processes for knowledge creation.

With respect to the Leibnizian view, Chapter 3 detected Leibniz's belief in formal logic and mathematical analysis for making inferences about cause-and-effect relationships. Organizations provide several resources to enable such knowledge creation by

a strict, formal, bureaucratic, "by the book" approach. Missions, policies, goals, and standard operating procedures serve as Leibnizian axioms. "Truth" is determined in a procedural manner, with focus on structural concerns, and with error detection and correction being a direct consequence of comparing inputs with the accepted "axioms" of the system.

Decision problems in a Leibnizian organization are attacked in a formal, analytic style. Mathematical models, especially optimization models that attempt to get at the one "best" answer, would be widely utilized.

(Courtney, 2001: 25–26)

The Lockean and Leibnizian organizational perspectives focus on how organizational members and groups are able to learn through data collection and analysis and through knowledge creation (model construction) to improve organizational decision making and problem solving. Knowledge-based systems have been developed in the past to support these processes. These systems consist of databases (see Chapter 2), models to calculate different decision scenarios (see Chapter 3 on quantitative models), and decision-making rules (see Chapter 3 on qualitative models). The integration of empiricism and rationalism, the ambition of Kant, thus is actually the same point, and indicates the need for knowledge-based systems, but when further studying the consequences of Kantianism (see Chapter 4),

I think that it also aims at reconciling different views on similar phenomena, something which is highly needed when multiple stakeholders are made responsible for organizational processes. I also stated in Chapter 4 that reference models and enterprise systems have the ambition to integrate the possibly different databases, models, expertises, and routines in an organization. This resulted in a shift from knowledge-finding individuals as the focus of information systems, to organizational processes and structures as the focal area. As a consequence, the systems that are part of the organizational resources from a Kantian view are not so much systems for individuals but enterprise systems for organizational knowledge integration.

The Hegelian view on information, as discussed in the previous chapter, emphasized the existence of information to support theses or antitheses in a conflict-resolution process of synthesis generation. The existence of conflicting views is an asset for organizations when the organization is also able to handle the dialectic processes well. This perspective on organizational information management has been summarized by Courtney as follows:

> This is a more complex decision style, as it is based on the fact that there is more than one perspective on the problem, and it specifically relies on the two most diametrically opposed perspectives. [. . .] The knowledge to be managed in this environment consists of the information that the thesis and antithesis attempt to interpret, the thesis and antithesis themselves, the debate, and of course, the synthesis.
>
> (Courtney, 2001: 27)

Competition and politics are the basic strategic realities of organizations, and negotiation and business systems, also named strategic information systems, are expected to support these strategic processes. These systems are able to handle conflicts of interests, i.e. the key aspect of the Hegelian approach.

Because these *knowledge-based systems*, *enterprise systems*, and *strategic information systems* consist of many different databases and software, the volume in investment in these systems may become many millions, and the daily support and exploitation may require a department by itself; IT infrastructure and IT capabilities management, for example, have become important, especially in larger firms (Weill and Broadbent, 2000). Therefore, IT resources have become a specific subject for management activities, i.e. the strategy and plan formation, development, exploitation in use, and evaluation and control cycle. The *continuous improvement ambition* is the ambition of a fifth epistemology. Edgar Singer's approach, which will be discussed in the next chapter. Table 6.1 summarizes the mentioned insights.

Until recently, the information management discipline was very much focused on supporting existing organizational structures and members with specific tasks, and as such information management work was divided

Table 6.1 Organizational aspects of information management

	Locke and Leibniz	*Kant*	*Hegel*
Information management objective	Data, models, and knowledge generation	Integration of models and data	Maximizing the competitive value of information
Information strategy	Realizing superior knowledge, intelligence, and expertise	Using information to realize well-integrated organizational processes and structures	Competitive advantage through excellent interactions with the business environment
Key organizational agent and organizational form	People and groups	Processes and structures	Top management and markets
Information systems type	Knowledge-based systems	Enterprise systems	Strategic information systems
Information technology support	IT infrastructure and IT capabilities management		
Evaluation for improvement	IS and IT evaluation methods		

along these functional applications. For the operating core, middle management, the apex, the techno-structure, and support staff, different types of information technological applications came into existence (Mintzberg, 1983). The requirements for these systems were derived from tasks in these units as summarized in Table 6.2.

The basic structures mentioned by Mintzberg are still alive in organizations, but a combination of changes in the market place and information technology has led to a search for further *integration of these organizational units by explicitly using information technologies* (Hammer and Champy, 2003). This means that the tasks, roles, and organization of the information management function have to be redefined in a broader sense as the *realization of new organizational capabilities* through IT strategizing, IT-enabled organizational structures and information systems, new information technological infrastructures, and constant improvement of IT capabilities by a critical evaluation of an organization's IT capabilities (see Figure 6.1).

Table 6.2 Organizational units, information system types, and their organizational function

Organizational unit	Information system type	Organizational requirements
Operating core	Order acceptance and delivery systems for sales and production	Supporting, quality improvement, and replacing jobs
	Expert systems for professional jobs	
Middle management	Monitoring and control reporting systems	Control processes and motivate people
Apex	Executive information systems	Support strategic analysis and communication tasks of executives
Techno-structure	Decision support and planning support systems	Support of advanced decision and management consultancy
Support staff	Administrative and accounting systems	Reducing transaction and administrative costs
	Groupware for supporting collaborative tasks in the office and research	Supporting internal vertical and co-lateral communications

Information systems strategy development

Organizations which excel in the management of IT and integrate IT well in the organization will have a competitive advantage. For instance, Davenport mentions the following successful cases of enterprise systems (ES) and new business processes.

Autodesk, a leading maker of computer-aided design software, used to take an average of two weeks to deliver an order to a customer. Now, having installed an ES, it ships 98% of its orders within 24 hours. IBM's Storage Systems division reduced the time required to reprice all of its products from 5 days to 5 minutes, the time to ship a replacement part from 22 days to 3 days, and the time to complete a credit check from 20 minutes to 3 seconds. Fujitsu Microelectronics reduced the

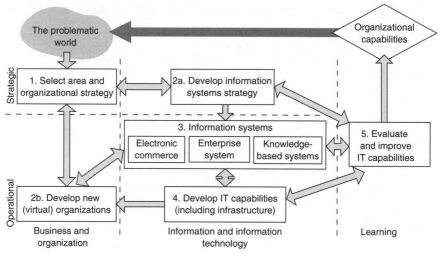

Figure 6.1 Information management processes.

cycle time for filling orders from 18 days to a day and a half and cut the time required to close its financial books from 8 days to 4 days.

(Davenport, 1998: 124)

Hansen *et al.* (1999) give Ernst & Young as an example, whose successful application of knowledge-based systems (KBS) resulted in high speed and efficiency of knowledge reuse. To illustrate this fact, they quote Ralph Poole, Ernst & Young's director of its Center for Business Knowledge:

After removing client-sensitive information, we develop "knowledge objects" by pulling key pieces of knowledge such as interview guides, work schedules, benchmark data, and market segmentation analyses out of documents and storing them in the electronic repository for people to use.

(Poole quoted in Hansen *et al.*, 1999: 108)

This approach allows many people to search for and retrieve codified knowledge without having to contact the person who originally developed it. These ideas aim at achieving scale in knowledge reuse and thus of growing the business.

To realize this level of information management, the literature often has argued in favor of information planning. *Information planning* distinguishes between information strategy, information architecture plan, and information project plan. Information planning uses a certain *planning horizon*, which may be short term (one to two years), middle to long term (two to four years), or longer term.

The *information strategy* and *information policy* plans are the responsibility of the most senior management in an organization. This management has to explicitly communicate the strategic directions of its information management including the technical, financial, social, and organizational constraints.

The *information architecture* plan further elaborates on:

- the technical infrastructure: this is the software for systems development and use, the type of hardware and network, the type of services that should be provided to users (like security, backup, and help desks);
- the data infrastructure needed: i.e. which databases are required and the need for connections or loose-coupling of databases;
- the systems architecture needed, and which systems will have what priorities for maintenance, developments, and replacement; and finally
- the organizational and human infrastructure of the IT organization, which may be centralized, decentralized, or deconcentrated: the organization of the IT department has implications for the responsibilities involved and the actual financial flows to realize information systems management processes.

The *project* plan or project portfolio is the part of an information plan, to realize a fluent flow of ideas from the strategic and architecture plan to the actual practical processes.

Information planning is a necessary activity for each organization. In the past top–down approaches dominated, which sometimes resulted in not listening to the needs of intended users, and often the poor communication of needs and opportunities of the IT department. Consequently, information planning was seen as not only the statement of goals and plans, but especially a *communication process* through which people coordinate and mutually adjust intentions and resources (Earl, 1996). The process is thus as important as the product or plan substance. These processes are often not predictable and therefore difficult to plan.

Developing new IT-enabled organizations

According to researchers in the area of organizational size and transaction costs, the inter-organizational communication facilities offered by the Internet enable strong reductions of *communication costs* and therefore the reduction of hierarchy in and among organizations (Venkatraman and Henderson, 1998). Consequently, *negotiated organizations* and *virtual organizations* nowadays frequently replace hierarchical firms and conglomerates. Such negotiated organizations require excellent designs of new business relations and the integration of physical and virtual value chains. Traditional organizational design variables will be supplemented and to some degree replaced by *IT organization design variables* (see Table 6.3).

Table 6.3 IT design variables

Type of design variables	Traditional design variables	IT-design variables
Structure	Definitions of organizational (sub) units	Virtual components, replacing for instance physical inventories by JIT-delivery and automatic ordering agreements
	Definition of goals and reports	Management reporting systems
	Linking organizational units	Electronic links like email and groupware
	Control mechanisms	Technological leveling, which enable management layers to be replaced and ease top–down and bottom–up interactions
Work process design	Task definitions	Production automation enables tasks to be executed by machines
	Workflows	Electronic workflows enable, for instance, a case or material to be processed by different people and be coordinated by software. Workflow management software is able to handle dependencies of different tasks, when the whole workflow is well modeled
	Buffers	Virtual components are able to reduce these buffers to planning and time problems and may reduce buffers to nearly zero
Communication	Formal channels	Electronic communication media supported by calendar systems and workflow control means

(continued)

Table 6.3 (continued)

Type of design variables	Traditional design variables	IT-design variables
	Informal communication and collaboration	Technological matrixing, which enables people to find each other easily and are able to electronically work on a same problem or case
Inter-organizational relations	Make-or-buy decisions	Electronic client–supplier relations facilitate purchase decisions
	Exchange of materials	Electronic client–supplier relations facilitate procurement processes
	Communication mechanisms	Electronic links to external media

Based on Lucas (1996).

With these IT organization design variables, four prototypically new organizations can be defined. Most attention in the literature has focused on the so-called *virtual organization*, an organization whose coordination mechanisms basically are electronically facilitated. This also implies that time and distance differences are bridged fully, so that people can work wherever they like (e.g. home, abroad, an office, and the airplane), and on each moment they like. They use IT intensively for communication and collaboration, for finding experts, and for management. This type of organization is typical for knowledge-intensive firms, such as consultancy and scientific institutes. A typical example is Compaq Computers' sales office. The physical Compaq sales office is nearly gone, because all the sales people operate from their own houses. Coordination of activities is realized via technological media. Electronic links and communications are very important to understand developments in the rest of the firm. Specific dates are planned for real-life meetings to develop and exchange *tacit* knowledge.

The *negotiated organization* consists of a collection of independent firms that realize a shared service by intensively exchanging product designs and client and delivery information. Because of the high interfirm dependencies, legal arrangements are vital to ensure the benefit of all (e.g. client data and other industrial intellectual ownership may be stolen and abused). This type of organization is typical for small high-tech firms that jointly develop new products, or have co-makership relations. This type is also typical for supply chain management cooperation, like the close links of agricultural product producers and their sales channels. An example is the Californian flower shop Calyx & Corolla.

> The California flower company Calyx & Corolla is based on two negotiated agreements. The first is with Federal Express to deliver flowers overnight to any destination in the United States at a favorable rate. The second agreement is with flower growers; instead of selling exclusively to wholesalers, the growers agree to put together a number of standard flower arrangements themselves. The final part of the organization is an 800-number and clerks to growers who prepare and address the arrangements for pickup and delivery by Federal Express.
>
> (Lucas, 1996: 39)

A less clearly recognized organization is the *traditional organization*, being fundamentally innovated by new IT potentials. These traditional organizations use IT intensively to improve the integration of business processes, to improve the efficiency and coordination of workflows, and to reduce the number of management layers and its costs. Prototypically they apply enterprise systems, and sometimes link these systems to the front-office (commercial) systems. Examples are the many organizations that adopt an executive information system with the purpose of improving (especially speeding up) top–down and bottom–up communication. This can enable the reduction of several management layers.

Classical types of advanced use of IT-design variables are the *vertically integrated conglomerates*. These are the large industrial firms that are able to force some standardization of IT applications upon their suppliers and subsidiaries, to improve the efficiency of its own processes. These vertically integrated firms are able to realize supply chain management systems, substantially reducing management and inventory costs.

Lucas (1996) examines the use of the IT-design variables per new organization type (see Table 6.4).

Information systems

Chapter 1 defined information systems in the limited sense of software systems and databases. Software systems process data according to a predefined purpose. This chapter has identified three types of information system. These systems will now be further explained.

Strategic information systems

Strategic information systems help us to handle the conflicts of interest between different stakeholders and organizations. This includes, among

Table 6.4 Four information technological organization prototypes

Organization design variable	Virtual organization	Negotiated organization	Traditional organization	Vertically integrated conglomerate
Virtual components	Substituted physical components	Substituted physical components	Used to replace isolated components	Forced onto suppliers and subsidiaries
Electronic links and communication	Essential part	Essential part	Difficult to use	Essential part
Technological matrix	Used by everyone	Used for coordination	Used by several groups	Used for coordination and task groups
Technological leverage	Used to monitor and support employees and independent work groups	Not applicable	Used to reduce the number of management layers	Used to reduce the number of management layers
Electronic work flows	Used as vital part of the strategy	Used as vital part of the strategy	Used where possible to reengineer work	Is crucial for the coordination of work unit activities
Production automation	Not applicable	Used for the communication of designs	Used everywhere where possible	Production coordination among work units
Electronic client–supplier relations	Extensively used	Extensively used	May be potentially important	Will become vital for operational activities

Based on Lucas (1996).

others, price setting on a market, negotiations between suppliers and buyers via an auction system, electronic commerce systems for the operational handling of business transactions, and systems for business intelligence and market research. This collection of systems is also often labeled electronic commerce, though the term electronic commerce systems mostly does not include business intelligence and market research.

Electronic commerce aims at

> the seamless application of information and communication technology from its point of origin to its endpoint along the entire value chain of business processes conducted electronically and designed to enable the accomplishment of a business goal. These processes may be partial or complete and may encompass business-to-business as well as business-to-consumer and consumer-to-business transactions.
>
> (Wigand, 1997: 5)

This definition suggests a technical and non-Hegelian nature of electronic commerce, but the rest of this subsection will explain the impact of electronic commerce on the power relations between buyers and suppliers. Therefore, I include electronic commerce in the broader class of strategic information systems.

A market transaction is a process of different, iterative tasks, which have to be conducted in order to exchange property rights. These tasks need supportive processes and institutions to realize low transaction, coordination, and search costs. The activities and institutions are given in Table 6.5.

Electronic commerce aims to reduce transaction and coordination costs among business partners by:

- the *communication* effect: IT allows more information to be communicated in the same unit of time, thus reducing transaction costs;
- the *electronic integration* effect: a tighter linkage between buyers and sellers is enabled;
- the *electronic brokerage* effect: an electronic marketplace where buyers and sellers come together to compare offerings;
- the *electronic strategic network* effect: IT enables the design and deliberate strategic deployment of linkages and networks among cooperating firms intended to achieve joint strategic goals.

By their virtual components, many strategic information systems replace inefficient intermediaries on the marketplace by *dis-intermediated* interactions (Wigand, 1997: 4). The previous intermediary roles, sometimes called middle men, brokers, or agents, may be replaced by an electronic market maker (like an auctioneer) or a value network (like common carriers and online market places), which in turn implies electronic *re-intermediation*. The extent to which intermediaries can be replaced by electronic means is

Table 6.5 Intermediary structures in e-commerce

Transaction activities	Intermediary structures	Example
I. Information: Market actors find information about other market actors	Transparency institutions define the visibility of other transactors' actions	Portals may help customers to find potential suppliers and vice versa
II. Order-routing: Market actors inform other market actors about their desire to conduct a market transaction	Access institutions define the quality of an order entering a market	A value network may define a certain format for orders for their system. A bank will require certain format and forms to accept the financial processing
III. Execution: Terms of the exchange are negotiated (like price and conditions)	Price discovery institutions define how price negotiations are conducted	An auction may apply a clock and a decreasing price in time. A market maker may allow space for bilateral negotiations about price and expenses of the transaction between maximally two interested parties (etc.)
IV. Settlement: The executed transaction is settled	Settlement institutions determine the settlement of executed transactions	This may include that a certain bank will arrange the money transfers, and also how the delivery of the good will be realized

Based on Picot *et al.* (1997).

highly dependent on the level to which *pre-execution expertise* is required. Picot *et al.* (1997: 114–115) therefore split *consulting-driven* from *execution-driven transactions*. An example of an execution-driven transaction is the booking of a flight. The transaction has dis-intermediation potential when the travel agency simply books the flight and provides no extra services. Consulting-driven transactions cannot be dis-intermediated because they rely on tacit knowledge that is not transferable. An example may be the underwriting of a life insurance policy. Product standardization is a way of making consulting-driven transactions execution-driven and potentially replacing the intermediaries.

Kambil and Van Heck (1998) distinguish trade processes from trade context processes (see Figure 6.2). The trade processes involve the search and valuation of offers from suppliers and buyers, the logistics for transporting

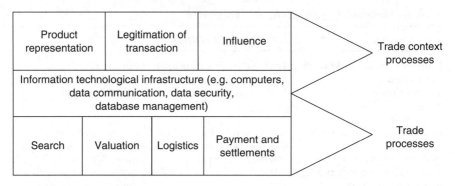

Figure 6.2 Exchange processes.

Based on Kambil and Van Heck (1998).

the goods, the payment and settlements (including the terms and the exchange infrastructure), the verification of the quality and features of the product offered, the authentication of the trading partners, and the monitoring of conformance to the contract or agreement among the parties. The trade context processes may consist of communication and computer support, product representation (applying, for instance, a standardized product and quality specification language), legitimization for the validation of exchange agreements, influence structures and processes to enforce obligations or penalties to reduce opportunism risks, and a legal or institutional structure to resolve disputes among parties.

Communication and computer technologies may have different roles for all these trade and trade context processes. Their potential impacts are summarized in Tables 6.6 and 6.7.

The acceptance of these technologies is highly dependent on the impact it has on the buyer and seller relationships. Some technologies may be more profitable for one of these parties and as such may be unacceptable. The type of impact may be split into impact on the direct *relations of buyers and sellers*, and impact on the *intermediary (market) structures*. The buyer–seller relationships can be IT supported already for many years by *Electronic Data Interchange* (EDI) systems, which enable electronic transactions within a clearly predefined contract between mostly two business partners. These business-to-business strategic information systems are mostly owned by one of the partners, who want to streamline its purchasing and reduce the transaction costs. Because of the high legal, financial, and operational impacts of such strategic information systems, formal contracts and very precise specifications of the trade are required. In business-to-consumer relations, enabled by a spread of the Internet among private persons, companies have new ways of presenting themselves to the public and giving consumers easier access to a

Table 6.6 IT impact on trade processes

Trade process	Potential IT impact
1. Search (I)	Search engines, portals, and electronic agents may reduce the search costs of potential offers. Electronic markets may help to find potential suppliers.
	Reduced role for intermediaries in finding suppliers. Sometimes the number of potential offers may be an overabundance, requiring new evaluation methods.
2. Valuation (III)	A variety of new price discovery means (electronic auctions, bidding processes, and negotiation via electronic agents) exist that differentially attribute costs to buyers, sellers, and intermediaries.
3. Logistics (IV)	When people don't buy via physical markets and outlets, the logistical problem of the delivery of small orders to client homes will be huge. New logistic intermediaries and a growing logistic service will come up.
4. Payment and settlements (IV)	Third parties may provide the infrastructures to reduce exchange risks, consisting of banking and legal services.
5. Authentication (II)	Third parties verify the quality and features of the product offered (certification). The authenticity of the trading parties in electronic commerce is required. Third parties may monitor conformance to the contract or agreement among parties, so that dispute resolution can be based on agreed data.

Based on: Kambil and Van Heck (1998).

Note
Roman letters refer to Picot's classification in Table 6.5.

company's information and services. These systems are basically an extra communication means, enabling transactions for very clearly presented products (with a homogeneous nature) and precisely specified trade terms. Because they do not require complex contracting processes, this type of strategic information system, called *Web commerce*, is quick and flexible. To reduce business uncertainties (a fundamental feature to motivate customers to buy), intermediary structures, like banks and courts, may have to be organized as well. The intermediary structure may be affected fundamentally by EDI and Web-based commerce systems. Many intermediary actors may be replaced, but also value networks and market makers may develop portals and electronic markets to facilitate buyers and sellers to exchange values. These market makers and portals replace physical markets and are called *electronic markets* here.

Table 6.7 IT impact on trade context

Trade context process	Potential IT impact
6. Communications and computing	Communications and computing processes bind all trading processes. Improved processing, storage, input–output, and software technologies transform the coordination and decision-making capabilities of stakeholders in each process. These transformations change the transaction costs and opportunity costs perceived by buyers, sellers, and intermediaries.
7. Product representation (II)	Product representation processes determine how the product attributes are specified to the buyer or third parties.
8. Legitimation (III)	Trade and exchange agreement can be validated online, by connections with credit card firms (which guarantee payment), checking authority of transaction by pin codes and membership numbers.
9. Influence structures and processes (I)	Explicit mentioning of the terms and conditions of the trade may reduce dispute problems, but only when existing, relevant legal and transaction data are available, reliable, and easily transferred to enforcement actors.
10. Dispute resolution (III and IV)	Probably legal institutes must be adjusted to settle legal problems in electronic commerce, but the law will need innovations and not much experience (jurisprudence) may exist yet.

Based on: Kambil and Van Heck (1998).

Note
Roman letters refer to Picot's classification in Table 6.5.

The actual application and impact of these information technologies are, however, limited by their (inter-)organizational aspects. Power relations among trade partners are rather decisive in this respect. In the case of EDI, mostly one powerful buyer is able to force a specific EDI system onto their suppliers, by applying the principle of "No EDI, No Business." In the case of the electronic market systems, the perception of a negative impact for one of the market partners may lead to a failure of the whole system. For instance, at the flower auction of Aalsmeer (Netherlands), one electronic trading system (Vidifleur) failed because the buyers felt that the electronic product representation led to a higher buyer risk whereas most of the profits of this system were to reduce the logistic and warehousing costs for the sellers and the auction itself (Kambil and Van Heck, 1998).

Electronic commerce systems may have particular misfit problems related to the lack of trust required in the market place, the poor alignment with the firm's market strategy, and a poor fit of these systems with operational processes in the organization. Table 6.8 gives some examples of typical misfits and potential solutions.

Strategic information systems in governmental and not-for-profit organizations are mostly not electronic commerce systems, because these organizations do not so much compete on operational efficiency or client services but may be in a direct competitive relationship with each other on access to scarce budgets or other resources. Having information about your competitor itself is in such cases an important asset. Consequently the strategic information systems of these organizations may contain information which is not disclosed to others or these systems have collected information about others and the market that may give executives a competitive advantage in negotiations. Such strategic data collection mechanisms are also named (business) intelligence systems or intelligence agencies. The organization and management of intelligence agencies has been described earlier by Wilensky (1967). Internal hierarchy, rivalry, specialization, and centralization seem to make these organizations often less effective. The increasing amounts that can be produced and reproduced by information technological support does not solve the difficulties of interpreting the gained data (actually more data often makes it worse) (Weick, 1979), and the disinformation intentionally produced by competitors is often hard to detect. Even if competitors are willing to share information, it may be hard to know what the competitor actually has and what the competitor does not present (this is the so-called information meta-game; Keck, 1987). Although I have stated that this strategic information issue is typical for government and not-for-profit agencies, these business intelligence issues are at least as relevant for company strategic policy making (Gilad and Gilad, 1988).

Enterprise systems

Enterprise systems are mostly used for the business process and management process integration (a Kantian epistemological issue). Taylorism, an organizational and managerial approach focusing on improving managerial control in organizations, is the major substantive foundation for the development of enterprise systems (also named enterprise resource planning systems or ERP). The core ideas behind Taylorism (Taylor, 1911) are:

- Business processes (or work) consist of several activities. There is mostly one best way for doing a job, which consists of a certain sequence of tasks, or some concurrency of tasks, leading to specific output in the most efficient way.
- The outputs of these processes have to be evaluated with regard to the goals set and the utilization of the resources. This requires all kinds of registrations, evaluations, control measures, and decisions to be taken (Beer, 1995).

Table 6.8 Misfits of strategic information systems and possible solutions

Causes of strategic information misfit	Examples of misfits	Potential solutions
Low transaction trust	Product under representation.	Add multiple media or physical observation locations.
	Unclear transaction terms.	
	Unclear partner identification and authentication.	Improve trade term representations on sites and develop legal services.
		Use trusted third parties.
Poor strategic alignment	Too efficient sales communications offering customers insufficient information.	Give sales force opportunities to intervene in case clients need more information or a more media-rich communication.
	Lack of customer–sales interaction leading to insufficient opportunities for customers to express their needs.	Let the E-commerce site not only be built to reduce costs but also to give added value in itself.
	Efficient interactions for transactions, but insufficient for relationship building and services.	
Poor system-operations fit (fit of electronic front office and back office)	Organization is unable to process high numbers of orders within promised term.	Check impact (e.g. by simulation) of E-commerce system on operational performance capacities.
	E-commerce orders are ambiguous to organization and/or client leading to high returns of goods shipped and claims.	Include clients in test periods (client acceptance test).

(continued)

Table 6.8 (continued)

Causes of strategic information misfit	Examples of misfits	Potential solutions
Poor information fit	Information overload and difficulty of interpretation. Competitor's disinformation. Hierarchy and bureaucracy blocks moving key information to the top. Incorrect information interpretation and filtering rules.	Reduce hierarchy and bureaucracy in intelligence units. Develop valid interpretation rules. Understand competitor's information disclosure behavior.

Because enterprise systems can only meet their high expectations when the basic information registrations and business models are in good shape (otherwise every systems output will be useless), business reengineering is often required in advance, parallel, or *ex post* of the ES implementation. The creation of the new Tayloristic symbiosis consequently requires a careful analysis of business model requirements.

The fundamental issue in operationalizing Taylorism is to model the *control system* as a *cybernetic system* (for vertical control; see Figure 6.3) and to model the *process flows* and related resources for horizontal control. The cybernetic systems consist of a control unit, an operations unit, and the information exchanges between them and the environment. The control unit receives messages of performance from the operation units. These data are compared with the control unit's objectives and directive messages are sent back to the operation units. Additionally, the control and operation units receive and send messages to external units. The control unit, for instance, receives messages from a superior authority and gathers and analyzes external messages to improve the control function (e.g. by modifying the objectives). The operational unit receives messages from (internal or external) clients (e.g. orders) and returns its acceptance of orders and bills.

Besides a flow chart (i.e. a set of interrelated activities), a well-managed business process also has resources like machines, materials, tools, buildings and space, knowledge, time, money, and available people. Enterprise systems attempt to manage these flows and stores together. This means that the cybernetic systems, which register and evaluate resources and their performance, are combined with the workflow management processes. This combination of resources and flows and their controls are described in Figure 6.4.

The idea of an enterprise system is nearly as old as the field of management information systems. Already in the 1960s several authors were actively engaged in developing information systems for managers to control

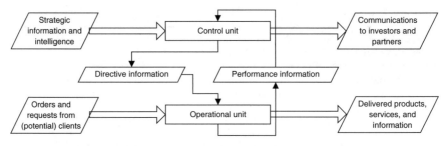

Figure 6.3 A model of a cybernetic system for vertical control.

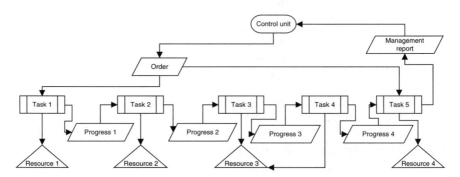

Figure 6.4 A workflow with five tasks (ending with reporting tasks) and four resources.

their business (Kirsch and Klein, 1977). In the beginning these information system concepts were going much further than what was technologically feasible, but in 1975 Orlicky for the first time marketed an information systems product that enabled some resources and materials management. The product was called Material Requirements Planning (MRP), and it was intended to support production planning within one firm and one plant by means of a computer and material resources capacity reporting. The basic concept in MRP was the bill-of-materials (BOM), which gives an exact list of materials to realize a certain product. By estimating the required product volume (orders), the demand for specific materials was calculated and purchase orders were created. Enterprise planning therefore was restricted to the planning of materials and storage needs, a necessary limitation given the expense of information processing capacity in those days.

At the beginning of the 1980s, MRP was extended to cover the planning of all production resources. This led to a much more integrated planning and management concept called MRPII, which stands for Manufacturing Resource Planning. Note the addition of the II, which marks the extension to materials planning which was the focus of the older MRP systems. Several current ES producers have their roots in those days, and extended their products from one of these resources (Kerr, 1990). SAP originated from materials and machine controls and People Soft from human resources.

All these MRPII products had their focus on the management of resources on one plant and location, but in the 1990s Just-in-Time deliveries and production as multi-local activities became an industrial requirement. As a consequence, the MRPII manufacturers extended their products to inter-firm resource planning and management. These products are called enterprise resource planning systems (ERP). In the second half of the 1990s, as a result of commercial globalization and the upswing of the Internet, these ERP systems not only served the bilateral interactions of two firms, but developed to serve the management of complete supply chains. These supply chain management systems are also called Extended ERP, and to a great extent merge with business-to-business electronic commerce.

All these ERP products offer their clients opportunities to manage relevant information, but more interesting is the knowledge they provide in terms of *best practices* for topics like stock replenishment, workflow routing, and priority setting of activities for scarce resources. A list of relevant modules, including expertise, for the SAP R/3 release is given in Table 6.9.

Although an ES package can facilitate integration among the organizational functions mentioned in the subsystems by a common database and modules in a shared software environment, it also may result in a further standardization of work practices among firms. According to Davenport (1998), this might lead to problems of strategic differentiation. Consequently, the implemented ES may have a large misfit with the current business strategy, management style, and business processes. To fit the ES and the business this mostly implies that the organization should fit in the system and not the other way round. Consequently, ES implementation also requires a far-going business process reengineering in advance or after the package implementation, but the risk of having a non-completed change process is large as well. For instance, Davenport (1998: 122) mentioned the case of Dow Chemical, where an ES implementation took seven years and cost over half a billion US dollars.

The problem of the ES-process misfits is caused by the fact that ES proposes a generic "solution" for process integration and quality problems. Through a well-grounded selection of modules, a match of a firm's needs and the ES opportunities can be created. The more modules are selected, the larger the scope of the realized implementation, and the more the integration of data and systems is achieved. SAP R/3 had about 3,000 configuration tables in 2001, which allows ES implementers to match the package to specific client needs. One example of this is the implementation of LIFO or FIFO principles for stock management.

A misfit between ES and the control structure in the firm can happen. An interesting example given by Davenport is the case of Hewlett-Packard (HP). HP has a strong tradition in local autonomy. Therefore, the

Table 6.9 SAP R/3 subsystems and modules

Subsystem	Modules
Financial	Accounts receivable and payable; asset accounting; cash management and forecasting; cost-element and cost-center accounting; executive information system; financial consolidation; general ledger; product-cost accounting; profitability analysis; profit-center accounting; standard and period-related costing
Human resources	Human-resources time accounting; payroll; personnel planning; travel expenses
Operations and logistics	Inventory management; material requirements planning; materials management; plant management; production planning; project management; purchasing; quality management; routing management; shipping; vendor evaluation
Sales and marketing	Order management; pricing; sales management; sales planning

Based on Davenport (1998: 122).

management has not forced high levels of commonality among the divisions with respect to ES implementation. This standardization was fundamental for financial consolidation, but for the rest HP kept its federal structure. This required much business modeling and process change to be done several times anew. This cultural conflict also may appear when looking at the management control structure. ERP, and specifically its management-reporting functions, may also help in moving information more efficiently up the hierarchy to create more centralization of power and less local democracy. This tendency of managerial control and centralization is also frequently mentioned in the literature on New Public Management by which ERP systems are sometimes described for the purpose of increasing control by managers over local production. This may sometimes result in less creativity and flexibility on the workfloor (Philippidou *et al.*, 2004).

This discussion of enterprise systems generated the organization and information systems fit–misfit issue of Table 6.10.

Knowledge-based systems

In many modern organizations, knowledge productivity has been recognized as the main factor for business success (Nonaka, 1994). Quite often it is possible to identify clear knowledge flows in organizations. In such organizations integration consists of combining knowledge in knowledge creation processes. Typical examples of such organizations are consultancy

Table 6.10 ES misfits and solutions

Misfit cause	Misfit	Possible solution
Inappropriate business model	Insufficient modeling of required connections between business activities	More details of models, especially with respect to communication needs
	Too high formality of order processing given interaction requirements with clients and suppliers	Allowing informality, and some under modeling (minimal critical specification)
Poor information management	Insufficient quality of data registrations	Data checking and administrative organization responding to top total quality management requirements
	Downtimes of mission critical modules	Redundant and fault tolerance of infrastructure
Context misfit	Users do not understand the underlying business model	Teach the business model or reduce its complexity
	Requiring personnel working times which are legally not allowed	Adjust model to incorporate constraints
	Requiring resource supplies which are environmentally and technically not feasible	Overcome constraints or adjust model
	Employees will behave less flexibly in fear of managerial control	Use ERP for the workfloor to improve their abilities of self-management

firms, teaching institutes, government administrative organizations, research organizations, and engineering organizations. The integration in such organizations happens in several ways:

1   One is the definition and communication of policies and priorities, which may be internalized by organization members and as such influences their behavior.

2   The other way is to analyze and externalize the existing knowledge, make it reusable (as explicit knowledge), and as such create a standard for the rest of the organization (e.g. method bases at Ernst & Young; cf. Hansen *et al.*, 1999).

3   The third way is to combine explicit knowledge, by defining links between documents and information systems and defining index and search structures for knowledge-containing systems.

4   The fourth way is to identify knowledge sources (without fully externalizing its contents) and link these sources with search means (e.g. skill databases).

5   Finally, nothing of knowledge description may be done at all, but nevertheless organization members may be given easy search and communication means to exchange ideas and problems and as such build up their expertise networks (thus the knowledge remains tacit).

All these knowledge integration features of a shared knowledge and information space are put together under the term of *knowledge-based systems* (KBS) (cf. Stein and Zwass, 1995). Besides Intranet software like Google, there are also more specialist packages to facilitate IT-based integration in this context, such as IBM's Lotus Notes, Open Text's Livelink, and MS SharePoint.

The number of applications and infrastructures needed for knowledge-based systems is very diverse. This is so because KBS integrate the Lockean and Leibnizian perspectives, i.e. database-related and model-oriented systems, and because KBS systems may be dispersed over many user groups and in fact often aim at group integration through space and time (Stein and Zwass, 1995). Binney (2001) mentions the following types of knowledge-based systems:

- transactional;
- analytical;
- asset management;
- process based;
- developmental; and
- innovation and creation knowledge management.

Collectively these elements are referred to as the KM (i.e. knowledge management) spectrum (Binney, 2001). The KM spectrum is a framework which covers all the KBS applications. In transactional KM, knowledge is presented to the user of the system in the course of completing a transaction or a unit of work, e.g. entering an order or handling a customer query or problem. In this case the knowledge is pre-packaged and provided to the user in the course of interacting with the system in a transaction to address a customer problem. Examples of transactional KM include help desk, customer service, order entry, and field support applications.

Analytical knowledge-based systems provide interpretations of, or create new knowledge from, vast amounts of disparate sources of material. In analytical KBS, large amounts of data or information are used to derive trends and patterns—making apparent that which is hidden due to the vastness of the source material and turning data into information. Traditional analytical KBS such as management information systems and data warehousing may analyze the data that is generated internally in companies (often by transactional systems). These analytical KBS often focus on customer-related information to assist marketing or product development functions. They are being joined by a range of competitive or business intelligence applications which incorporate external sources of knowledge or information. Such competitive intelligence applications are being used by companies and government agencies to analyze and understand what is happening in their market place and assess competitive activities. Scenarios are the most common method used here. For instance, if one needs to provide quick answers to complex questions such as "What are my competitors doing to take advantage of the Net?"

Asset knowledge-based systems focus on processes associated with the management of knowledge assets. This involves one of two things:

1   The management of explicit knowledge assets which have been codified in some way.
2   The management of intellectual property (IP) and the processes surrounding the identification, exploitation, and protection of IP.

Once captured, the knowledge assets are made available to people to use as they see fit. This is analogous to a library, with the knowledge assets being catalogued in various ways and made available for unstructured access and use.

The process-based knowledge-based systems cover the codification and improvement of processes, also referred to as work practices, procedures, or methodology. Process-based KM is often an outgrowth of other disciplines such as total quality management (TQM) and process reengineering. The knowledge assets produced in this category are also known as "engineered assets" in that they often involve third parties or specialists working with practitioners or subject matter experts to document these best practices in standard formats. Process knowledge assets are often improved through internal lessons, learned sessions, formal engineering of the process by internal best practice selection, and codification and external benchmarking.

Developmental knowledge-based systems focus on increasing the competencies or capabilities of an organization's knowledge workers. This is also referred to as investing in human capital. The applications cover the transfer of explicit knowledge via training interventions, or the planned development of tacit knowledge through developmental interventions such as experiential assignments or membership in a community of interest.

Investing in developing the knowledge and capabilities of a company's workforce is becoming a measure of the value of an organization because this investment is now seen as increasing the knowledge content and capability of an organization. At the same time, such investment also helps to attract the best knowledge workers in a highly competitive knowledge worker market. There is an emerging emphasis on developing "learning organizations" and collaborative skills. Communities where people can exchange ideas and learn from each other is another emerging form of tacit knowledge development.

Innovation and creation-based knowledge-based systems focus on providing an environment in which knowledge workers, often from differing disciplines, can come together in teams to collaborate in the creation of new knowledge. There is still a role for individual innovation; however, innovations are increasingly coming from the marriage of disciplines and teamwork. The focus of the business and KBS here is on providing an environment in which knowledge workers of various disciplines can come together to create new knowledge. The most common application referenced in the literature is the creation of new products or company capabilities.

There is a phenomenal growth of technologies that make it easier to implement KBS. These technologies continue to evolve rapidly, especially in the areas of collaboration and search engines. This evolution, combined with the pervasive nature of and access to Web-based technologies, is "enabling" the KBS, which are a number of technologies which underpin most of today's KM applications and cannot be primarily assigned to only one element of the spectrum. These have been called "pervasive technologies." They include Internet/Intranet technologies and generic Web elements such as portals. These pervasive and underpinning technologies are listed in Table 6.11.

A number of IT and organizational developments are required to develop the spatial and temporal integration and the ideal KM-situation (see Table 6.12).

Whereas traditional organizations group people together at the same physical location for efficient knowledge sharing, several IT variables enable knowledge management. Consequently, much of the notion of an office is being replaced by electronic mail, video conferencing, and other Internet-based groupware. This relieves many people of having to travel between office and home, which may be particularly problematic in high-congestion areas. It also allows for more organizational flexibility, because everyone with an Internet connection may be facilitated by electronic access codes and software to enable knowledge sharing and knowledge creation with people who have never had face-to-face interaction before. Of course, knowledge management leads to new managerial challenges, because it may be hard to have the shared understanding needed for effective knowledge sharing when people have never met face to face before.

Table 6.11 Knowledge-based systems and enabling technologies

Types of KBS	Example systems	Enabling technology
Transactional	Case-based reasoning; helpdesk systems; customer service applications; order entry systems; service agent support systems	Expert systems; cognitive technologies; semantic networks; rule-based systems; rule-induction systems; geo-spatial systems
Analytical	Data warehousing; datamining; business/competitive intelligence; management information systems; decision support systems; customer relationship management systems(CRM)	Intelligent agents; web crawlers; neural computing; database management systems; data analysis and reporting tools
Asset management	Intellectual property management; document and content management systems; knowledge repositories	Search engines; knowledge maps; library systems
Process based	Process automation; best practice management systems; bench marking tools; quality measurement and assessment tools	Workflow management; process modeling tools
Developmental	Teaching, training, and simulation systems; Competence management systems; electronic Human Resource Management systems	Computer-based training development tools; serious game development technologies; online training facilities
Innovation and creation	Communication, collaboration, and discussion forums; virtual team management systems; expertise networking tools	Groupware; email; chat rooms; video conferencing; search engines; bulletin boards; information services (e.g. EBSCO)

Based on Binney (2001).

IT infrastructure and its development

The concept of IT infrastructure and capability

IT infrastructure is the platform, i.e. the technical and human IT foundation, on which the business applications can run. Figure 6.5 gives a model of the IT environment, which describes the business application and IT infrastructure elements, and arrows denoting places of linkages for possible integration.

Table 6.12 Misfits of KBS and organization

Level of integration	Organizational developments	IT developments	Examples of misfit
Temporal integration	People need time and resources to store. They should be motivated in expectations of reuse. The stores need professional support to maintain continuity of its existence.	Indexed databases of events, problems, and designs possibly enriched by multimedia.	Large archives with low utilization. No learning from the past. No formalization of experience where possible. The IT systems offer a lot but the people cannot use it.
Spatial integration	People should be willing to publish and inform others. They need facilities to realize knowledge transfer (especially between SBUs and firms). Settling of ownership disputes.	Shared databases and knowledge bases. Shared distributed work templates, as part of groupware systems.	"Reinventing the wheel" problem. Poor intergroup collaboration in knowledge creation. Not knowing about knowledge available to others.
Ideal	Intelligence creation process and organization to strategically tune the organization with the environment. Knowledge sharing and creation with partners. Being able to make decisions with utilizing past experiences and all experts wherever they are. Finding the right people and maximum reuse of expertise. Reducing the costs of routine decisions.	Systems to support adaptation, inter-organizational knowledge creation, and goal-attainment. Systems for social knowledge structure transparency (yellow pages, etc.). Systems for electronically handling rules and values (admin systems and WFM).	Repetition of above.

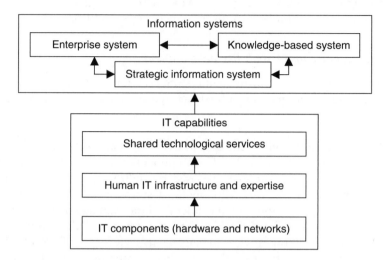

Figure 6.5 Information technology management elements: Systems and supportive IT capabilities.

Source: Based on Weill and Broadbent (2000).

Weill and Broadbent (2000) define an IT infrastructure as the basis for the planned IT capacities (technical as well as human), which are shared resources in a firm via reliable services and mostly managed by the information systems and technology group of the firm. The bases of the infrastructure are the IT *components* like computers and communication technology, which are available as commodities on the market place. On top of this basis layer is a second layer, containing shared *services* like the management of large-scale data processing, creating electronic data interchange (EDI), and the management of business-wide databases. Weill and Broadbent mention the following IT services required for running its business applications: (1) data communication management; (2) application management; (3) data management; (4) management of standards; (5) IT education management; (6) IT services management; (7) security; and (8) IT research & development (R&D). The IT components are used and transformed to meaningful services via its *human IT infrastructure*; which contains knowledge, skills, and experiences.

Each of these layers of the IT infrastructure has its opportunities and limitations. These may be related to problems with its interactions with other IT components (for instance, because a new IT component may be based on a different technological standard than the other IT component), the interaction with the human IT infrastructure (for instance, the IS group may lack the knowledge, time, and means to install, maintain, and manage the new technology), or the organization may lack the services required to have the new component or application run successfully (such as, lacking processing capacity, a network with poor qualities, insufficient security measures, and lack of disaster-recovery schedules).

IT infrastructure and capability development

IT infrastructure development requires the creation of its services, IT components, and its human IT infrastructure, such that the following can happen:

1   The IT infrastructure elements fit well with each other. According to Weill and Broadbent (2000), IT components (software, hardware, middleware, networks, etc.) can be used by skillful people (the human IT infrastructure) to realize the following IT services: communications management, applications management, data management, standards management (for hardware operating systems and data communications), IT education, services management, security, and IT R&D. These eight services may fit or misfit each other's requirements and the IT strategy.

2   The IT infrastructure fits well with the systems it is expected to support. ES, strategic information systems (SIS), and KBS require that the IT infrastructure realizes a certain level of *reach* and *range*. Reach refers to the locations and people the infrastructure is capable of connecting. Reach can extend from within a single business unit to the ultimate level of connecting to anyone, anywhere. Range refers to functionality in terms of the business activities that can be completed and shared automatically and seamlessly across each level of reach. ES, SIS, and KBS have different requirements here.

3   The IT infrastructure fits well with the organization strategy. A Nolan and Norton survey among sixty-seven IT executives from three different continents showed that often the *alignment* of IT and corporate goals is hard to accomplish. One of the reasons for this is the lack of a common language between the IT and organizational stakeholders involved in such a policy-making process. In the past, money, in terms of return-on-investment, was often thought to provide a common language, but unfortunately it was in fact too restricted and the consequences of IT investments for ROI were too indirect (Soh and Markus, 1995). Van der Zee and De Jong (1999) therefore introduced the balanced score card as a tool in creating effective IT strategic alignment. This balanced score card instrument requires the stakeholders to answer key questions with respect to the financial perspective, customer perspective, business processes, and organizational learning. The balanced scorecard approaches a full integration of IT and business development, because it allows IT and business people to speak the same language. The discussions result in cause-and-effect diagrams, which represent these shared views. A self-explanatory example of a bank is given in Figure 6.6.

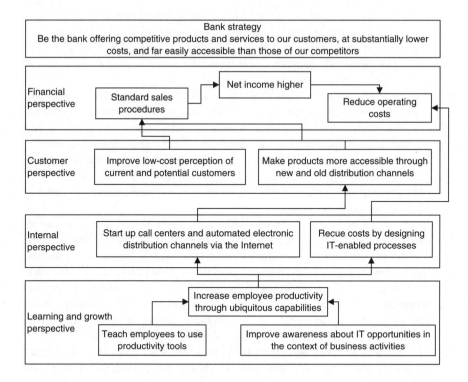

Figure 6.6 A cause-and-effect diagram for the application of score card concepts in vision creation.

Source: Van der Zee and De Jong (1999: 149). Reprinted with permission of M.E. Sharpe.

The IT capability of a firm consists of all technologies and its management: an enterprise-wide capability to leverage technology to differentiate from the competition. To be able to exploit these capabilities fully, it is required to understand what makes up this construct of *IT capability*. Bharadwaj *et al.* (1999) detected six dimensions of the IT capability construct based on a two-stage Delphi study with IT management experts from academia, consultancy, and industry. These six categories are:

1   *IT business partnerships.* The dimensions here refer to a firm's ability to foster rich partnerships between the technology providers (IT professionals) and technology users (business unit managers). IT includes aspects related to the blending of business and IT experience through multi-disciplinary teams and encouraging risk sharing and experimentation with IT. This relationship building also enables the user's understanding of IT's potential. The IT business partnership construct can be measured by: existence of multi-disciplinary teams to blend

business and technology expertise; relationship between line management and IT service; line management sponsorship of IT initiatives; a climate that encourages risk taking and experimentation with IT; a climate nurturing IT project championship; and IT-related educational initiatives for management.

2   *External IT linkages*. This dimension refers to technology-based linkages between the firm and its key business partners, including customers and suppliers. Inter-organizational IT like EDI networks and electronic distribution channels facilitate these sophisticated networks. External IT linkages can be measured by: technology-based links with customers; technology-based links with suppliers; the use of IT-based entrepreneurial collaborations with external partners; and leveraging of external IT resources.

3   *Business IT strategy thinking*. This dimension refers to the management's ability to envision how IT contributes to business value and the ability to integrate IT planning with the firm's business strategies. Indicators for its measurement are the following: clarity of vision regarding how IT contributes to business value; integration of business strategic planning and IT planning; management's ability to understand the value of IT investments; funding for scanning and pilot-testing "next generation" IT; and technology transfer mechanisms.

4   *IT business process integration*. This dimension refers to the ability to adapt existing business and IT work processes to continually enhance their effectiveness as well as to leverage the capabilities of emerging information technologies. It requires the restructuring of existing business practices as well as the restructuring of existing IT work processes to ensure that new opportunities for process efficiency are exploited. The construct can be observed through: checking the consistency of IT application portfolios with business processes; the restructuring of business work processes to leverage opportunities; and the restructuring of IT work processes to leverage opportunities.

5   *IT management*. This dimension taps into activities related to the management of the IT function, such as IS planning and design, IS application delivery, IT project management, and planning for standards and controls. This leads to the following observation dimensions: effectiveness of IT planning; IT project management practices; planning for security control, standards compliance, and disaster recovery; systems development practices; consistency of IT policies throughout the enterprise; IT evaluation and control systems; and adequacy of the skill base.

6   *IT infrastructure*. In other words, the services, components, and human IT capabilities.

IT and IS evaluation

There are many issues that should be evaluated about the quality and value of an organization's information resources. In 1989 Kumar (Kumar, 1990) performed a still-interesting survey where he asked his respondents to state how frequently they used a list of IS evaluation criteria. On the basis of a factor analysis, these criteria fit well in three dimensions:

1 *Information criteria.* Accuracy of information, timeliness and currency, adequacy, and appropriateness of information.
2 *System facilitating criteria.* User satisfaction and attitudes toward the system, internal controls, project schedule compliance, quality and completeness of documentation, net operating cost-savings, security and disaster protection, hardware performance, and system performance versus specification.
3 *System impact criteria.* System usage, user-friendliness, the system's impact on users and jobs, and the system's fit with and upon the organization.

Although this is a rather complete list of IS evaluation criteria, some of these criteria will be more important in certain contexts, depending on the role given to the evaluation. The importance of IS evaluation has been mentioned frequently, but the frequency of evaluations done in practice is rather limited. Kumar's survey mentioned that 20.9 percent of the respondents stated they had never conducted an IS evaluation, 14.3 percent stated that between 1 and 24 percent of the systems were evaluated, 26.4 percent stated that between 25 and 49 percent of the systems were evaluated, 8.8 percent stated that between 50 and 74 percent of the systems were evaluated, and 29.7 percent stated that 75 percent or more of the existing systems were evaluated. In 27.8 percent of the cases, the evaluations were conducted just before system delivery. In 4.2 percent of the cases this was done at the moment of delivery. The other percentages are 22.2 percent (after one month), 6.9 percent (after two months), 18.1 percent (after three months), 1.4 percent (after four and five months), 13.9 percent (after six months), and 4.2 percent (after twelve months).

Lack of time, qualified personnel, and knowledge, the political sensitivity of evaluations, and insufficient expected benefits explain why IS evaluation is often not done.

Because people as part of administrative and managerial processes are error prone, the idea occurred that machines would be principally non-erroneous, and as such the quality of these processes would increase by computer applications. Of course, computers did not solve all these errors, because the designers, data entry agents, and system users were still people and as such errors still occurred. The quality of the information supplied by computer systems could be incorrect, incomplete, non-current, imprecise,

Table 6.13 Information systems-facilitating evaluation criteria

Dimension	Systems-facilitating criteria
Information systems development process	1. Quality conditions (available skills; project management methodology; systems development methodology; roles in project); 2. Quality controls in IS project; 3. Continuity in IS project; 4. Completeness of services in the project (i.e. training and documentation); 5. Third-party development/outsourcing
Features of the information system and documentation	1. Flexibility; 2. Maintainability; 3. Testability; 4. Portability; 5. Connectivity with internal and external systems; 6. Reusability; 7. Quality and fit with the infrastructure
Information systems user performance	1. Reliability (correctness; completeness; permissibleness; currency); 2. Continuity (availability; robustness; recovery; upgrading opportunities; fall-back arrangements); 3. Efficiency (speed; user-friendliness; cost efficient; connection link with manual procedures; efficiency of manual procedures); 4. Effectiveness (coverage; availability through time and space; usability; decision support; support of end users)

and non-verifiable. The causes for this may be in the areas of the system development process, features of the information systems, or the system's performance. Consequently, several system-facilitating criteria emerged in the last decade. These are summarized in Table 6.13.

Organizational scientists have also added the issue of the impact and contributions of information systems in terms of their organizational functions, i.e. (1) contributions to the organization's strategic objectives, (2) improvement of the efficiency of primary processes, (3) improvement of organizational adaptation and learning, and (4) improvements to the organization's financial success (cost-benefit). Kaplan and Norton (1996) have codified these interests into the so-called *scorecard method* of IS evaluation.

Although an interesting list of evaluation categories can be named from this quality perspective, they all fit within the constraints of the *dependent view*, which implies that "investments are primarily intended and tailored toward a particular business strategy" (Weill and Broadbent, 2000: 339). This means planning, evaluation and investments of IT only can be taken after the current business strategies have been articulated.

Alternatively, the *enabling view* regards IT as a value in itself, being a vital part of a firm's core competence, and as such integrated with the strategic context of the firm. This requires extensive infrastructure capabilities, increasing the strategic options and agility. Enabling infrastructures often require expanding the reach and range of infrastructure components. The flexibility of the infrastructure enables a number of as yet unspecified business strategies to be implemented more rapidly than firms with a dependent or utility view of infrastructure (Weill and Broadbent, 2000: 340).

The dependent and enabling views of IT differ markedly from the *utilitarian view* on IT infrastructure. These views on IT infrastructure have large implications on their IT investment levels, assessment criteria, and the reach and range and services of their infrastructure.

Method of information management

The previous section explained that from an organizational and strategic perspective certain ways of getting hold of information systems and IT infrastructures are needed. We can summarize the related methods as below:

1   Develop information system strategies:

    1.1   Identify and understand the corporate and business strategy.

    1.2   Identify the implications of the organization's strategy for organizational design variables (see Table 6.3).

    1.3   Develop IT organizational prototypes (see Table 6.4).

    1.4   Select information system types (i.e. SIS, ES, and KBS) that should help realize the IT organization prototype.

    1.5   Develop an enterprise architecture by using the ArchiMate method, as presented in Chapter 4.

2   Analyze the required information systems and assess their fit with the organization.

3   Develop the IT infrastructure and capabilities:

    3.1   Describe services and IT components to support the information systems.

    3.2   Check how the required level of reach and range can be realized.

4   Evaluate: Specify IS and IT evaluation criteria and how these can be used in improving the information systems and infrastructure.

Reflective practice

This chapter clearly is not as easily related to any kind of everyday individual experience, but has an organizational focus. This focus has identified the resources an organization can deliver for realizing the ambitions of the philosophers mentioned earlier. The method presented above, though, summarizes information management issues which are valid for any organization. The reader may like to find out how the following organizational contexts have to be supported by offering organization.

- How do you think an Internet e-commerce shop will have to organize issues around its systems? Just imagine any e-commerce shop on the Internet (e.g. Amazon.com) and how it will have to cope with strategies, the type of systems its services need, the IT capabilities required, and their evaluation mechanisms.
- An interesting case is E-lance, a service which provides skills for specific tasks and a mechanism for matching tasks and suppliers of skills. How would the strategies, systems, and IT capabilities for E-lance differ from Amazon.com?
- In the government area, consider what has to be arranged for a safe and sure passport delivery service.

Discuss these examples and make your own information management manual based on your reflections over the three examples given (or any other you agree on in your virtual group).

Further reading

Elementary further reading on IS strategy and organization and tasks of the ICT department

Kroenke, D. M. (2008) *Experiencing Management Information Systems*. Upper Saddle River, NJ: Pearson Prentice Hall, pp. 37–48, 69–90, 256–296, 451–482, and 559–583.

On organizational perspectives of epistemologies

Courtney, J. (2001) "Decision making and knowledge management in inquiring organizations: Toward a new decision-making paradigm for DSS," *Decision Support Systems*, 31: 17–38.

On organization

Hammer, M. and Champy, J. (2003) *Reengineering the Corporation: A Manifesto for Business Revolution*. New York: Harper Business Essentials (first printed 1993).

Lucas, H. C. (1996) *The T-Form Organization: Using Information Technology to Design Organizations for the 21st Century*. San Francisco: Jossey Bass.

Mintzberg, H. (1983) *Structures in Fives: Designing Effective Organizations*. Englewood Cliffs, NJ: Prentice Hall.

On IS strategy

Rayport, J. F. and Sviokla, J. (1994) "Managing in the marketspace," *Harvard Business Review*, 72, November–December: 141–150.

Van der Zee, J. and De Jong, B. (1999) "Alignment is not enough," *Journal of Management Information Systems*, 16(2): 137–156.

Venkatraman, N. and Henderson, J. C. (1998) "Real strategies for virtual organizing," *Sloan Management Review*, Fall: 33–48.

On strategic information systems

Kambil, A. and Van Heck, E. (1998) "Reengineering the Dutch flower auctions: A framework for analyzing exchange organizations," *Information Systems Research*, 9(1): 1–19.

Picot, A. and Bortenlanger Heiner, C. (1997) "Organization of electronic markets: Contributions from the new institutional economics," *The Information Society*, 13(1): 107–123.

Wigand, R. (1997) "Electronic commerce: Definition, theory, and context," *The Information Society*, 13(1): 1–16.

On enterprise systems

Davenport, T. (1998) "Putting the enterprise into the enterprise system," *Harvard Business Review*, July/August: 121–133.

Kerr, R. (1990) *Knowledge-Based Manufacturing Management: Applications of Artificial Intelligence to the Effective Management of Manufacturing Companies*. Boston, MA: Addison-Wesley.

Scheer, A. (1998) *Aris: Business Process Frameworks*. Heidelberg, Germany: Springer.

Taylor, F. (1911) *The Principle of Scientific Management*. New York: Harper & Sons.

On knowledge-based systems

Binney, D. (2001) "The knowledge management spectrum," *Journal of Knowledge Management*, 5(1): 33–42.

Earl, M. (2001) "Knowledge management strategies: Toward a taxonomy," *Journal of Management Information Systems*, 18(1): 215–233.

Nonaka, I. (1994) "A dynamic theory of organizational knowledge creation," *Organization Science*, 5(1): 14–37.

Stein, E. W. and Zwass, V. (1995) "Actualizing organizational memory with information systems," *Information Systems Research*, 6(2): 85–117.

On IS/IT evaluation

Doll, W. and Torkzadeh, G. (1988) "The measurement of end-user computing satisfaction," *Management Information Systems Quarterly*, 12(2): 258–275.

Kaplan, R. and Norton, D. (1996) *The Balanced Scorecard: Translating Strategy into Action*. Boston, MA: Harvard Business School Press.

On IT capability management

Bharadwaj, A., Sambamurthy, V., and Zmud, R. (1999) "IT capabilities: Theoretical perspectives and empirical operationalization," *Proceedings of the 20th International Conference on Information Systems*, Charlotte, North Carolina, pp. 378–385.

Weill, P. and Broadbent, M. (2000) "Managing IT infrastructure: A strategic choice," in R. Zmud (ed.) *Framing the Domains of IT Management: Projecting the Future . . . Through the Past*. Cincinnati, OH: Pinnaflex.

7   The Singerian view and information management research

Introduction to Singerian epistemology

The need for pragmatism

There are many research methodologies which quite well correspond to the philosophies of knowledge that we have presented before. The Lockean epistemology, for instance, is not only important as a basis for understanding databases but gives a foundation for descriptive *empirical research* as well. The Leibnizian epistemology is not only a foundation for (decision) support modeling, but it is important for scientists in the *positivist* and formal logical traditions, which both aim(ed) at finding law-like statements about the world. The Kantian epistemology tried to integrate the Lockean and Leibnizian ideas and aimed at a *multi-view* integration. This is also consistent with the use of multiple research methodologies in one study (Mingers, 2001). Hegel's work on understanding the motives behind informative expressions and dialectic logic is consistent with so-called *interpretive* and *critical* approaches in the social sciences and management information systems (MIS) field (e.g. Klein and Myers, 1999; Walsham, 2005). For information systems research, interpretive and critical research has an important place in its ambitions of realizing solutions which can be well understood and accepted by its user organization.

Churchman (1971), Mason and Mitroff (1973), and Courtney (2001) all agree that there is one philosophy which integrates the four epistemologies in a pragmatic way, named the Singerian or pragmatic epistemology. The Lockean, Leibnizian, Kantian, and Hegelian approaches all aimed at finding the truth. Especially the Leibnizian view is very explicit here, because Leibniz believed in an ultimate truth, which is owned by the "architect of the universe," i.e. God, and man is ambitiously trying to uncover more and more pieces of this truth. Locke has a more relaxed ambition, because he sees knowledge much more at an empirical level, i.e. attempts at detecting important regularities in observations and sharing these contingent truths in a community of interested people. For him explanations and predictions are of course also important, but attempts at trying to find the ultimate truth is regarded as over-ambitious and achieving consensus between people over how they see the world is already a quite great achievement. Kant is a bit more optimistic with regard to digging below the surface of observations, and detecting more fundamental categories for explaining facts. Knowledge, however, in Kant's view, is the result of people who learn and combine their insights to larger bodies of knowledge. Hegel introduces an additional human element in truth detection: the existence of different and competing views, and the usefulness of discussion to achieve "higher" truths, named synthesis. Although the idea of people aiming to find absolute truths is much criticized, still aiming at it is regarded as a *value-in-itself* according to all four. The Singerian approach, in contrast, states that the continuous search for new and improved truths is important, but only valuable as far as it results in human *progress*.

Churchman understands Singer's epistemology as a continuous search for improvements for mankind. He summarizes the Singerian perspective in the following nine elements of an inquiring system:

1   The inquiring system has the purpose of creating knowledge, which means creating the capability of choosing the right means for one's desired ends.

2   The measure of performance is to be defined as the "level" of scientific and educational excellence of all society, a measure yet to be developed.

3   The client is mankind, i.e., all human teleological beings.

4   The components have been the disciplines, but the design of inquiry along esoteric, disciplinary lines is probably wrong, as we have seen, if the purpose is "exoteric" knowledge, i.e., knowledge that goes outward to be useful for all men in all societies.

5   [. . .] Singer's theory of value is essentially "enabling." That is, ethical values are based on an assessment of man's capability of attaining what he wants, and not on an assessment of the goals as such. [. . .] the environment which the inquiring system critically needs is a cooperative environment, where A wants that goal which will aid B in attaining his goal. [. . .]

6   The decision makers are everyone—in the ideal. But at any stage there will be the leaders and the followers. For Singer the most important decision makers are the heroes, those inspired by the heroic mood to depart from the safe land of the status quo. [. . .]

7   and 8. The designers are everyone—in the ideal. Progress can be measured in terms of the degree to which the client, decision maker, and designer are the same. [. . .]

9   I have purposefully stressed the theme of betterment in the foregoing account, even to the point of a kind of simplistic optimism. [. . .][1]

(Churchman, 1971: 200–201)

Obviously, multi-disciplinary work and the participation of many people, including academics and practitioners, under heroic leaders, is needed to improve mankind. Scientists are part of the game, but not the only participants, but society expects its scientists to work in an *interdisciplinary* way and in close *collaboration with problem owners*, who have a clear stake in improving the *human condition*.

Singerian epistemology and design science

Singerian inquirers seek a highly idealistic purpose, the creation of *exoteric knowledge*, or knowledge for "every man," as opposed to scientific, esoteric knowledge that, as it matures, becomes relevant to an increasingly smaller audience. The artificial division of knowledge into disciplines and the reduction of complex problems into simple components inhibit the solutions to social and management problems. Solving complex problems may require knowledge from *any* source and those knowledgeable in *any* discipline or profession.

Attempts to achieve such a kind of pragmatic exoteric knowledge has substantial organizational and human consequences. The Singerian organizations must bring in multiple perspectives or world views in their thinking and decision-making processes.

> A critical aspect of developing multiple perspectives is open, honest, effective dialogue among all relevant stakeholders in the problem involved. Managers in such an environment must be careful to respect the rights and viewpoints of the parties involved, and be open and honest to themselves in order to gain the trust of those who will be affected by the decision.
>
> (Courtney, 2001: 28)

The Singerian approach develops multiple perspectives in several ways, as Courtney states:

> First, [. . .] the system "sweeps in" the other thinking styles, which means it uses any or all of them where appropriate in decision-making processes, and may include any knowledge as needed from any discipline or profession to assist in understanding the problem. [. . .] All complex problems—especially social ones—involve a multiplicity of actors, various scientific/technical disciplines, and various organizations and diverse individuals. In principle, each sees a problem differently and thus generates a distinct perspective on it.
>
> (Courtney, 2001: 29)

In "real-life" situations, managing problems consists of at least (a) analyzing alternatives, (b) making decisions about which alternative to choose, and (c) successfully implementing the chosen alternative. The Lockean, Leibnizian, Kantian, and Hegelian perspectives focus most strongly on (a) and least on (c), hence the "gap" so often deplored between analysis and action.

Successful implementation depends first and foremost on the use of human resources and this means that we have to move from (a) to (c).

> In developing organizational perspectives, parties in the decision-making process often fall into camps that advocate a preferred alternative, with each camp seeking to develop ammunition to support its position. Also, each camp tends to base its position on unstated assumptions which, if left uncovered, often lead to a circular debate that gets nowhere. For example, Mitroff and Linstone give the example of a pharmaceutical company that was trying to decide what to do about competition from a generic drug that was a substitute for its largest selling product. One camp argued that the price should be raised, the other that it should be lowered. Each was making an unstated assumption about the behavior of physicians. One believed that prescribing physicians would assume that the higher price meant higher quality and would prescribe the pharmaceutical companies' product. The other believed that physicians were cost conscious, and that the company had to compete on a cost basis. Surfacing such assumptions is a critical part of developing organizational perspectives. Mitroff and Linstone suggest that assumptions can be surfaced by first identifying all stakeholders (anyone or group affected by the decision) and then simply asking each camp what they have to assume is "true" of a particular stakeholder such that starting from that assumption that camp's preferred policy or actions would be supported. Of course, in complex, social decisions there will be many diverse stakeholders, some of which may have overlapping members, such as various special interest groups, taxpayers, governmental agencies, businesses and so forth. Surfacing assumptions about all these stakeholders may not be an easy task.
>
> (Courtney, 2001: 29–30)

The consequences of the Singerian approach are not only organizational in an abstract sense, but also concrete in the attitudes and behavior of individual organization members. Kienholz *et al.* (1993) therefore have developed the *Inquiry Mode Questionnaire* (InQ), which measures an individual's propensity to use the different inquiring styles described by Churchman. The *Synthesist* (Hegel) appreciates conflict, and is capable of integrating information from opposing views. The *Idealist* (Kant) employs multiple, but analytic, views, seeks ideal solutions, and values both data and theory. The *Analyst* (Leibniz) uses models, formulas, and formal techniques to derive "optimal" answers. The *Realist* (Locke) prefers data and facts to theory, and seeks concrete results. The *Pragmatist* (Singer) is open to multiple perspectives, is innovative and adaptive, and is best in *complex situations*.

Knowledge of thinking styles can be helpful in seeking input from individuals with different ways of looking at decision problems. This will help to ensure that multiple personal viewpoints are represented, rather than getting input from several who think alike. Even more, it helps in delivering substantial complementary knowledge and opinions needed to understand and manage complex challenges. Managing the diversity of the related capabilities is key for effective information management.

Singerian pragmatism is a major epistemology for information management, which is not so much interested in understanding any laws (Leibniz' ambition) or regularities (Locke's ambition) about information management itself, but very much is a discipline aiming at *changing and improving the world by the many new opportunities information technology provides to us*. The scientific challenge thus cannot simply be the development of new truths via testing or development of theory, but the *research process* will have to realize a close interaction between real-world problems of problem owners and the body of knowledge existing in the field. This is aimed at by integrating multiple perspectives, and so information management scientists will have to cope with many *theories*, not only technical and social, but both. Figure 7.1 gives a key model of the Singerian epistemology as an integration effort of scientific rigor and practical relevance (i.e. esoteric and exoteric knowledge), which is a generalized version of the *pragmatic science model* introduced in Chapter 1.

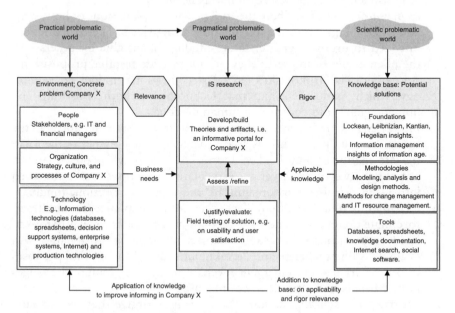

Figure 7.1 The design science model of information management.

Source: Based on Hevner *et al.* (2004).

Consequently, design science (Hevner *et al.*, 2004) is the root model for information science. Design science aims at understanding the problematic world of an individual or organization, selecting appropriate theories and methods to possibly solve the problems in a *learning project*. This learning project thus has information from the problem context and relevant theories and methods as input, used to construct a solution, which is tested next. After the testing, the conclusions are drawn by delivering advice to the problem context and possibly amending the theories available. We will further describe this design approach, and the nature of design theory and the processes involved in design science research.

MIS theories

Following Gregor (2006), theories in the information systems field can be classified as follows with regard to their goals:

1   *Theories for analysis and description.* These theories systematically describe a phenomenon, without any attempt to explain or predict. An example is Iivari *et al.* (2000), who propose a dynamic framework for classifying information system development approaches and methodologies. Other examples are classifications of information systems, and Churchman's classification of inquiring systems on the basis of the philosophers we have described in this book.
2   *Explanatory theories.* These theories provide explanations of how, why, and when things happened, relying on varying views. These theories are intended to promote greater understanding or insights by others into the phenomena of interest. They do not provide testable propositions. An example is Orlikowski's (1992) structurational model of technology, which made the claim that technology is both constituted by human agency and constitutes human practice.
3   *Predictions.* A prediction is a theory which states what will happen in the future if certain preconditions hold. An example of a predictive theory in the information systems field is Moore's law (1965), which proposes that, as technology evolves, larger and larger circuit functions can be crammed into a single semi-conductor substrate, meaning costs continue to fall.
4   *Explanation and prediction.* These theories use explanatory theories to formulate predictions, and the explanations consist of explicitly formulated propositions which can be subject to empirical falsification. An example is Bhattacherjee and Premkumar's (2004) theory that proposes causative drivers and emergent mechanisms driving temporal changes in user beliefs and attitude toward IT usage.
5   *Theory for design and action.* These are prescriptive theories, actually often of a predictive kind, when the prediction is that the use of a certain method or technique will result in some wanted goal. An example is Markus *et al.*'s (2002) theory, which prescribes certain methods, tech-

niques, and design actions for developing information systems that best suit emergent (i.e. changing and less formal) knowledge processes.

In design theory, the first four types are named "kernel theories," whereas the design theories are "a prescriptive theory based on theoretical underpinnings which say how a design process can be carried out in a way which is both effective and feasible" (Walls *et al.*, 1992: 37). Such design theories consist of integrated prescriptions of a particular class of user requirements, a set of system solutions, and a set of effective development practices (Markus *et al.*, 2002: 180). Walls *et al.* (1992) distinguish product-oriented and process-oriented design theories, to be discussed next.

MIS product-oriented design theories

Product-oriented design theories focus on *features of the end product*, i.e. provide *meta-requirements* and *meta-designs* that help to solve classes of problems and create classes of artifacts. We follow Walls *et al.* (1992: 42) here: ". . . we use the term 'meta requirements' rather than simply requirements because a design theory does not address a single problem but a class of problems." For example, for an information service (which is a set of IT and human means to inform people, like an electronic newspaper or a bank's website for its investment clients), this implies the specification of content, use features, and revenue mechanism requirements, knowledge of which is necessary in order to make the service effective as an intermediary between content suppliers, information goods consumers, supportive service providers, and sponsors.

With respect to meta-designs, Walls *et al.* (1992: 42) "use 'meta design' because a design theory does not address the design of a specific artifact (e.g., a payroll system for XYZ corporation) but a class of artifacts (e.g., all transaction processing systems)." A meta-design for information services describes the set of components (i.e. databases, organizational structures, and information technologies) and relations between them, according to which (sub)systems for information services can be designed. These designs may be expressed in design architectures covering the different layers and their relations (Jonkers *et al.*, 2004; Sowa and Zachman, 1992).

Product-oriented design theories require kernel theories and design propositions (Markus *et al.*, 2002). A kernel theory consists of propositions that explain what components are useful, how they can be related in a system, and why they serve the requirements. A kernel theory also may explain the requirements that are most suitable for a given situation or actors. For information services, the kernel theory may explain the impact of the design contingencies on the service design products. Product-oriented design hypotheses have propositions that empirically link meta-requirements to meta-designs. If the design hypothesis is incorrect, any design built according to this design theory will show mismatches with agreed or aimed-at requirements.

If an information service aims to be informing, and if all the philosophers we have discussed in this book have relevant insights for informing, each philosophy may be a kernel theory pointing at different requirements and design aspects. The Lockean kernel theory may emphasize the need for data and content and its careful specification and structuring. The Leibnizian kernel theory may point at delivering useful models, which clients can use to analyze, modify, or select content by which their value experiences increase. This is what we call *use value features*. The Kantian kernel theory focuses on integrating the content and use features by specific processes of acquisition and delivery of the content and the features. The Hegelian kernel theory may emphasize the existence of different stakeholders and ways of settling the differences to form a business model which is acceptable for all key players (clients, content and features suppliers, possible sponsors, and the service management). The organizational view of Courtney may emphasize the need for a supportive organization and infrastructure for the service. Finally, the Singerian kernel theory may emphasize the need for adopting and improving the service based on experiences, new opportunities, and evolving client needs. The resulting design characteristics of information systems are summarized in Table 7.1.

Each design aspect requires precise specification of its requirements. If these requirements are well documented and argued, and when its criteria for effectiveness have been well described at the beginning of an information service design process, the requirements can be a useful baseline for the rest of the design project. Requirements have to be specified such that they can be shared and understood by relevant stakeholders and unambiguously assessed or measured at the end of the development project. This is not only in the interest of the project clients but also of the project management, who do not want to have disagreements at the end about the intentions of the project (which may result in dissatisfied clients and even clients not willing to pay the bill for the project). Such requirements specification should at least include the definition of the goals of the system, its rationale, and the quality and system behavioral characteristics aimed at. An interesting template for the requirements specification is given by the Volere method (see www.systemsguild.com/GuildSite/Robs/Template.html; accessed May 4, 2008). Also the PRINCE2 approach for project management gives clear instructions here (see www.prince2.com).

MIS process-oriented design theories

For accomplishing a design process, designers may use specific *methods and techniques* for representing and analyzing their impressions related to each design layer. They also need *design scenarios*, i.e. prescriptions of how their design work has to evolve from start to finish, with different sequences among the layers and aspects, in one sequence, or through iterations.

Table 7.1 Kernel theories and design aspects for information services

	Kernel theory (explanadum and explanans)	Information service design aspect	Comparable information systems
Locke	Communicative and consensual; empiric	Data repositories; data models; input forms and query and reporting tools; content aspect	Databases
Leibniz	Causalities; formal, analytic models	Decision support models; implemented decision support tools and user interfaces for improved user content value; use value aspect	Decision support systems
Kant	Multi-facet reality; integrated analytical models	Cross-functional work support by implemented process and organization models; integrated submodels and modules; organizational process aspect	Integrated KBS and workflow and process management systems
Hegel	Conflicts; understanding ethical differences and settling differences	Collaborating stakeholders of an information service; Internet query and triangulation tools; business model aspect of content and service	Internet triangulation tools and information system business models
Organization theory (Courtney)	Organizational context of information; means and infrastructure analysis	Information policy, information systems, and information service infrastructure; information service policy and means aspect	Information service infrastructure

(continued)

Table 7.1 (continued)

	Kernel theory (explanadum and explanans)	Information service design aspect	Comparable information systems
Singer	Learning and progress; multi-disciplinary problem solving	Improving service through research, analysis, and improvement actions; maintenance and exploitation aspect	Group problem-solving systems

Design scenarios

Two approaches to information system development scenarios exist, which have a tremendous impact on the way and opportunities of realizing new IT-organization symbioses. These approaches are called "in-house development" and "third-party development" (outsourcing). The differences of these approaches are made manifest by a survey of Gasson and Holland (1995) among 49 firms. The differences in these approaches indicate that in-house development is more people-oriented and the third-party development is more technology-oriented (see Table 7.2).

These differences in the use of user participation tools have major consequences for the creation of the IT-organization fit. Low use of user participation, for instance, has severe consequences for user understanding of the broader context and intent of the information systems introduced. Often it may be a cause for resistance and poor acceptance. Of course, this may easily happen while using external developers, who will not so easily understand the organization's technology and context, but internal IT experts may fail for the same reasons. Therefore a more fundamental determinant for poor IT-organization fit is the project management method applied. The related project management approaches are described by Gasson and Holland by applying elements of Leavitt's diamond for socio-technical design (see Table 7.3).

Methods and techniques

A *process-oriented* design theory prescribes kernel theories, design methods, and research propositions with regard to the process of design. As part of the process kernel theory for information service design, we take the information systems insight that design requires a few steps from abstract goals to concrete means. These steps are named design layers, and range from understanding the economic and social goals of a system (part of the business model) to its realization in concrete technical means (the infrastructure). Between goals and infrastructure, business process models are

Table 7.2 Ranking of user participation tools

User-participation tool	In-house development	Third-party development
Participation of users as development team members	81%	47%
Joint design with users	63%	6%
User training in development tools	34%	6%
Use of evolutionary system prototypes	31%	0%
User workshops to discuss design changes	50%	18%
User-directed testing schedules	75%	18%
User-redesign of work processes	28%	18%
Modifications to system design to support business applications	63%	47%

Source: Gasson and Holland (1995: 223). Proportion of respondents using highest-ranked user-participation tools at each stage of the systems development life cycle.

often constructed to operationalize a business model to service actions (Hedman and Kalling, 2003). Knowing these actions enables a designer to select the appropriate means to facilitate and support these service processes. The joint collection of means for these processes is named the (information service) infrastructure (Weill and Broadbent, 2000). Walls *et al.* (1992) and Markus *et al.* (2002) mention three *parts* of a process design theory in addition to the kernel theory, i.e.

1   the methods and techniques that are advised to be used for doing the requirements analysis and design work;
2   the work scenarios that coordinate design tasks; and
3   process design propositions, which explain or predict empirical relations among design process variables on the basis of the design process contingencies (context and objectives).

As part of the process design theory, the design steps may be done with different levels of intentionality, in sequences or iterations, depending on the complexity and uncertainty of the project.

Table 7.3 Six dimensions of IS-development approaches

	Leavitt's model	Operationalized concepts
	Hard	Soft
Technology-structure	Technical optimization	Work and social system design
Technology-people	Low user participation	High user participation
Technology-task	Top–down, technical approach to problem investigation	Bottom–up, task approach to problem investigation
Task-people	Function-oriented approach to system design	Work-process-oriented approach to system design
Structure-people	Formal, system specification orientation to development project management	Informal, user-satisfaction orientation
Task-structure	Long, waterfall approach to systems development	Short, evolutionary approach to systems development

Source: Gasson and Holland (1995: 217).

To illustrate the idea of process-oriented design methods and techniques, we use the development of information services as an example. The design layers can be executed by using different methods and techniques for each layer (e.g. Sowa and Zachman, 1992). The following design *layers* can be identified (see Chapter 4):

1　problem and agenda setting;
2　business and process requirement identification and analysis;
3　design of the infrastructure;
4　construction of the prototype; and
5　exploitation and evaluation.

Exploitation and evaluation, although often suggested to fall outside the scope of the design process, are regarded as essential elements in information service design, because it is often difficult to know in advance what the actual needs of the information market are. The client group is geographically often dispersed (sometimes all over the globe), and consequently a market analysis in advance may be too superficial (Albert *et al.*, 2004). The development of a system for monitoring client needs is therefore a critical design layer (Palmer, 2001). Consequently, we split the exploitation design (e.g. selecting key performance indicators and ways of analyzing the performance data) from the actual evaluation and feedback. Table 7.4 shows the methods and techniques for each layer.

Table 7.4 Methods per design layer

Design layer	Process kernel theory	Method
1. Project problem and agenda setting	Hegel	Stakeholder analysis and problem charts
2. Business requirements	Leibniz	Requirements specification
3. Process requirements	Kant	Process diagrams and integration of work activities
4. Construction	Kant	System architecture design; relations between databases, use interfaces, and applications
5. Design propositions	Locke	Empirically testable causal relations between problems, requirements, and design components
6. Organizational support	Courtney	IT business alignment model and organization chart of the IT function
7. Exploitation and exploration	Singer	Analysis of system use behavior

Layer 1: Problem analysis and agenda setting

A well-known lesson of information system development projects is that before one starts it must be clear that the project has sufficient support from key stakeholders. This implies that a *stakeholder* identification is required and that each stakeholder need must be well analyzed, i.e. it should become clear that a sufficiently large collection of stakeholders have similar positive opinions about the project so that they will supply the resources needed for the project. A *causal analysis* of what would happen if the problems were not solved by an information service is an important tool for communicating about the problem with stakeholders (Gregor, 2006). Such a causal model also helps to scope the project by stating what causes will be part of the project. For example, in most cases not all causes can be solved or treated by an information service. The stakeholders can have an important say in the priorities of what can be coped with and what the actual goal variable must be.

Figure 7.2 gives the key stakeholder roles of an information service (the content and use feature supplier, the content and use feature consumer, the sponsor, and support services such as the Internet service supplier and software supplier) and the information service manager. These actors exchange content, use features, and revenues (not necessarily only financial).

Layer 2: Business requirements specification

Because information services are intermediaries between stakeholders (i.e. suppliers, users, sponsors, and support providers), the existence of an information service depends on its ability to enable value exchanges between these stakeholders, which results in sufficient satisfaction for all to become members of the business network. Consequently, the kernel theory for information services at the business level is value nets (Gordijn and Akkermans, 2001). The *business requirements* can be represented in a business model, which is a (explicit or tacit) business proposal for all actors involved in an information service. Some actors deliver or collect content, user features, and revenues. Some of these are required and others are optional for a successful service. Thus, a viable information service must have a business model that specifies what stakeholders have to deliver in return for what, and this business model must realize sufficient means to (at least) cover the costs of the information service.

Sponsors are often important for realizing information services (Womack, 2002), but attempts by information services to raise advertising incomes may result in clutter costs, which are fictive prices for the consumers.

The business requirements for a possible music service are given in Figure 7.3, using the *E3 Value method* (Gordijn and Akkermans, 2001; www.e3value.com). This E3 Value model gives a further specification of the general stakeholder model of Figure 7.2. Each actor in the E3 Value model must be sufficiently compensated for his or her efforts, to realize the whole business network. If one actor sees insufficient merit in participating, the business model will not be feasible.

Layer 3: Process requirements specification

Regarding the *process requirements*, an information service delivers content, facilitates content use, and collects revenues. These processes are interlinking mechanisms between the network actors. Three core processes interlink the activities of the actors:

1   Ordering and delivering, which can be content logistic or content transformation. Content logistic activities consist of acquiring, storing, and delivering of content. Content transformation improves content value on top of what the supplier delivered to the service by

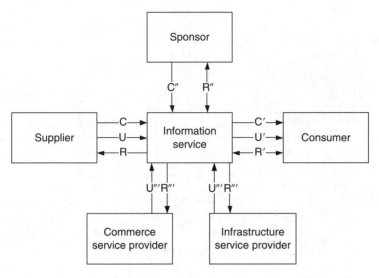

Figure 7.2 Information service stakeholders and their exchanges.

Note
C = content; U = use features; R = revenue.

modifying the information good's representation level (reducing over-load) and its conceptualization (reducing cognitive distance and misunderstanding e.g. by delivering extra background information). The related process models are named content service models. These service models can be presented by content–user interactions.

2   An information service may deliver use content facilitation to its cus-tomers by providing content interaction means and meta-information (e.g. quality indicators) about the content. To know what interactions have to be supported, use support models can be created by use case and task descriptions.

3   Transaction processing compensates suppliers and external use facilita-tors and collects funds to cover the service's costs by applying rules concerning quality demands and performance. The related process mod-els we name transaction processing models. A good transaction processing model also works explicitly with the revenue rules stated in the business model, i.e. that it accesses client bank accounts for payments. This must of course be defined very precisely in terms of prices per con-tent and use units, use measuring mechanisms, and billing procedures.

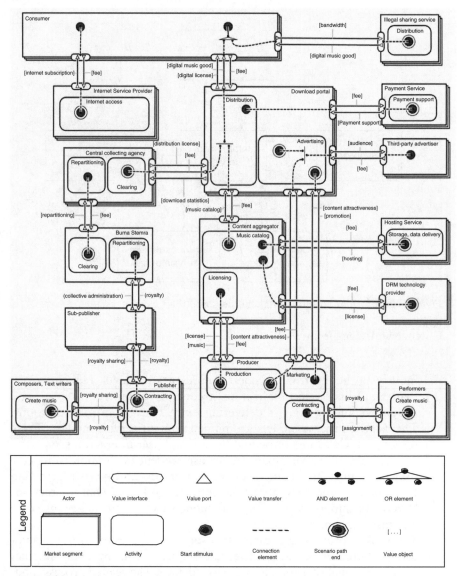

Figure 7.3 The E3Value business model for a music download portal.

Source: Voermans (2007). Reprinted with permission of Koen Voermans.

Layer 4: Construction

For the infrastructure layer, knowing the process activities will facilitate the determination of the informational, human, and information technical means. For the design aspect (content, value, and revenue) different models are needed. For content we have to describe the data precisely in data structures and entity relation diagrams (see Chapter 2). For content interactions, we need to specify interfaces, which intersect content and use. For the use aspect, we need activity diagrams as further elaborations of use cases, which next can be used to denote relevant IT applications and their relations in an architecture model (e.g. ArchiMate; see Jonkers *et al.*, 2004), and organizational tasks and their relations in an organization chart. For revenue we need to formalize the payout rules, and we need data collection mechanisms to find out if certain payout rules should be activated.

For information services, content management systems are ready-to-use software easing the realization of information services. These content management systems offer authoring, search, navigation, content structuring (and indexing), and subscription-handling use features. Some of these content management systems are even freely available via the Internet, like Drupal and Joomla! (see http://drupal.org and www.joomla.org).

Layer 5: Design propositions

Following the Lockean approach, we have to empirically validate our design results. This implies that all the main means–goals relations in our design should be interpreted as causal hypotheses. Next, data has to be found to critically evaluate any relation between means and goals in the design. For an information service in general this has been done in Figure 7.4.

Layer 6: Designing the service's organizational support

The information service management can take different roles and tasks. Bourhis *et al.* (2005) outline these in Table 7.5.

Following Bourhis *et al.* (2005), different roles need to be taken for virtual communities depending on the community's demographics, organizational context, membership, and technological characteristics. The reader is referred to their paper for details, but there is no "one-size-fits-all" solution for the management roles of information services. The reader may also have noticed in Chapter 6 of this book that internal organizational affairs of information management are complex, because they require the alignment of business strategies, organizational structures and processes, information systems, and the information technological infrastructure.

Layer 7: Exploitation and evaluation

Exploitation requires the definition of performance indicators, the specification of methods and tools for the analysis of performance data, and the specification of ways on how the resulting *behavioral* insights can be used

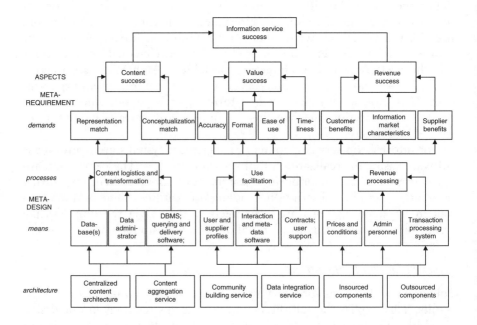

Figure 7.4 Design propositions for an information service.

Source: Wijnhoven and Kraaijenbrink (2008). Copyrights owned by Fons Wijnhoven and Jeroen Kraaijenbrink.

Note
Each arrow denotes a hypothetical causal relationship.

for feedback. With respect to indicators, the use of log data may be essential. Any kind of market research, for instance, gives a too-superficial and expensive feedback to the designers (Albert *et al.*, 2004). To be effective here, a log information collection and organization mechanism is useful, named the log information architecture (Albert *et al.*, 2004). Transaction log analysis mostly requires substantial data cleaning before it can be actually done. The current literature on informative Web performance has delivered a few interesting performance measures as well. For instance, Palmer (2001) has developed and validated the following measures: download delay, organization/navigation, information/content, interactivity, and responsiveness. Yang *et al.* (2005) identify and validate five measures, i.e. usability, usefulness of content, adequacy of information, accessibility, and interaction. The exploitation and evaluation layer aims at insights that might help improve the service by the following methods:

Table 7.5 Information service management roles

	Role	Description
Knowledge domain roles	Subject matter experts	Keepers of the community's knowledge domain or practice; centers of specialized tacit knowledge
	Core team members	Develop the community's mission and purpose
	Community members	Take active ownership in the community by participating in its events and activities
Leadership roles	Community leaders	Provide the overall guidance and management needed to build and maintain the community
	Sponsors	Nurture and provide top-level recognition for the community
Knowledge intermediary roles	Facilitators	Network and connect community members by encouraging participation
	Content coordinators	Ultimate sources of explicit knowledge by searching, retrieving, and transferring explicit knowledge, and responding to community requests
	Journalists	Identify, capture, and edit relevant knowledge
Community support roles	Mentors	Act as elders for the community, help new members to navigate in the community, and set norms and policies
	Admin/event coordinators	Coordinate, organize, and plan community events or activities
	Technologists	Oversee and maintain the community's collaborative technology and help members navigate its terrain

Based on Bourhis *et al.* (2005).

1   Behavioral analysis through (log) data collection and analysis of actual use and performance of the service.
2   A logical reflection about how the design process actually has evolved and if everything which has been created in each layer is consistent with the other steps. Reviewing the kernel theories, requirements, infrastructure design, and actual realization in the prototype can result in important insights for further design theory development.

Information management research topics for e-government and e-business contexts

There are many interesting subjects for research in the information management field, and the easiest way for getting some overview here is to check the indexes of the top-level journals in these fields. Some of these journals are listed below:

- *Management Information Systems Quarterly*
- *Journal of Management Information Systems*
- *Communications of the ACM*
- *Information Systems Research*
- *Journal of Strategic Information Systems*
- *Electronic Commerce*
- *Information and Management*
- *European Journal of Information Systems*
- *Information Systems Journal*
- *Internet Research*
- *Journal of the Association for Information Systems.*

For more journals and resources also see www.home.aisnet.org/ association/7499/files/index_Markup.cfm.

Management Information Systems Quarterly also has a special journal for executives named the *MISQexecutive*. This journal publishes the main information *technological* concerns, which for 2005 are listed below, with priorities mentioned by 105 top managers between brackets:

- IT and business alignment (1)
- Attracting, developing, and retaining IT professionals (2)
- Security and privacy (2)
- IT strategic planning (4)
- Business process engineering (5)
- Introducing rapid business solutions (6)
- Measuring the value of IT investments (7)
- True return on IT investment (7)
- Complexity reduction (9)

- IT governance (10)
- Project management capabilities (10).

This list is interesting because it helps to set a research agenda with high practical relevance. It should be noted that this list is focused on *technologies*, which is only one part of the information management infrastructure. The other part of this infrastructure consists of the people and organizational resources. Information management involves more than only the selection and realization of efficient infrastructures. Maybe more important are the processes of handling the information and effective strategies of creating value by using information. This book has focused on these processes and touched on the infrastructure just a little. A more complete picture, though, should also comprise business strategies and the alignment of information management processes and infrastructure with these business strategies (see Figure 7.5).

Figure 7.5 demonstrates that the relations between business strategy and organizational and IT infrastructure have developed many insights in the last few decades, but that it lacks some insights related to information procedures from an understanding of what information and informing stands for. There are many research challenges on the intersections of information handling with organizational infrastructure and business strategy, which at the moment still require substantial new research, preferably from a design science perspective.

Reflective practice

Some readers may argue that the contribution of science to a much-changing discipline as information management is quite limited and sometimes even misdirecting. Indeed, the "body of knowledge" of our discipline is large, and finding relevant content which is of the proper *rigor* to be able to make an innovation is often difficult. This means that practitioners need good mechanisms for finding appropriate knowledge, and discussion with the "body of knowledge" experts (academics) in that case is needed. These "body of knowledge" experts also really should try to make a practical contribution, i.e. make a *relevant* contribution. I believe very much in Singer's statement that good academic work should be "exoteric" and thus be useful for everyday life. It also should be rigorous, i.e. academic statements must be well grounded on what we think is true, building on an academic tradition, and really contributing to this. We also advise the reader to read Webster and Watson (2002) for multiple good ideas of how to detect a useful contribution. In practice, though, attempts to realize "exoteric" knowledge need the contribution of several disciplines, and the task of meta-information management, being the job of integrating the insights from these disciplines and practical insights as well, is the key for successful project management. A simple assignment to look at the challenge of meta-information management is outlined on the next page.

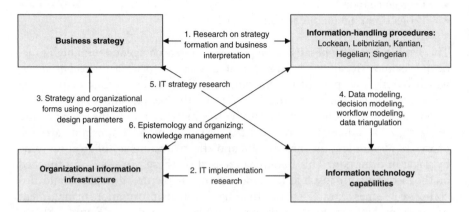

Figure 7.5 Information management research issues in the context of information alignment.

- Select a topic from Figure 7.5.
- Collect articles on these topics in international scientific journals.
- Make a data model and database for e-gov and e-business research for these topics and their article titles, and insert abstracts in the database.
- What can be found on the Internet about these, given the use of key terms from the database?
- Which universities seem to deliver major research in these areas?
- Which consultancy firms have profiled themselves on these topics (and how)?
- Which organizations seem to have the chosen topic as a key challenge?
- Define queries and reports.
- Discuss the Internet as a knowledge resource versus university library resources.
- Write a report concerning the experiences of your virtual learning group in this assignment.
- Why study informing instead of information technology?

Further reading

Further elementary reading on design science

Kroenke, D. M. (2008) *Experiencing Management Information Systems*. Upper Saddle River, NJ: Pearson Prentice Hall, pp. 517–557.

On Singer

Churchman, C. W. (1971) *The Design of Inquiring Systems: Basic Concepts of Systems and Organization*. New York: Basic Books.

Courtney, J. (2001) "Decision making and knowledge management in inquiring organizations: Toward a new decision-making paradigm for DSS," *Decision Support Systems*, 31: 17–38.

Kienholz, A., Hayes, P., Mishra, R., and Engel, J. (1993) "Further validation of the Revised Inquiry Mode Questionnaire," *Psychological Reports*, 72(1): 779–784.

Mason, R. and Mitroff, I. (1973) "A program for research on management information systems," *Management Science*, 19(5): 475–487.

On MIS theory

Gregor, S. (2006) "The nature of theory in information systems," *Management Information Systems Quarterly*, 30(3): 611–642.

Hevner, A., March, S., and Ram, S. (2004) "Design science in information systems research," *Management Information Systems Quarterly*, 28(1): 75–105.

Iivari, J., Hirschheim, R., and Klein, H. (2000) "A dynamic framework for classifying information systems development methodologies and approaches," *Journal of Management Information Systems*, 17(3): 179–218.

Walls, J., Widmeyer, G., and El Sawy, O. (1992) "Building an information system design theory for vigilant EIS," *Information Systems Research*, 3(1): 36–59.

On process-oriented design theories

Albert, T., Goes, P., and Gupta, A. (2004) "GIST: A model for design and management of content and interactivity of customer-centric web sites," *Management Information Systems Quarterly*, 28(2): 161–182.

Gasson, S. and Holland, N. (1995) "The nature and processes of IT-related change," in *Information Technology and Changes in Organizational Work. Proceedings IFIP WG 8.2 Working Conference*. London: Chapman & Hall, pp. 213–234.

On information management research issues

Luftman, J., Kempaiah, M., and Nash, E. (2006) "Key issues for IT executives 2005," *Management Information Systems Quarterly Executive*, 5(2): 81–99.

Webster, J. and Watson, R. (2002) "Analyzing the past to prepare for the future: Writing a literature review," *Management Information Systems Quarterly*, 26(2): XIII–XXIII.

On information services

Bourhis, A., Dube, L., and Jacob, R. (2005) "The success of virtual communities of practice: The leadership factor," *The Electronic Journal of Knowledge Management*, 3(1): 23–34.

Wijnhoven, F. and Kraaijenbrink, J. (2008) "Product-oriented design theory for digital information services: A literature review," *Internet Research*, 18(1): 93–120.

Notes

1 Introduction

1 Source: www.plunkettresearch.com
2 Source: http://finance.yahoo.com/q?s=MSFT
3 Source: http://finance.yahoo.com/q?s=CSCO

2 The Lockean view and databases

1 This description of John Locke is based on the Wikipedia page on John Locke (March, 2008), Uzgalis (2007), and Churchman (1971).

3 The Leibnizian view

1 This description of Leibniz is based on the Wikipedia page on Leibniz (March, 2008), Look (2008), and Churchman (1971).
2 For this tutorial see the Microsoft website at http://office.microsoft.com/en-us/visio/HA010837201033.aspx.
3 For more information about Excel's decision-making functions, have a look at www.comfsm.fm/~dleeling/exceltraining/advexcel.html.

4 The Kantian view and multiple perspectives

1 This description of Immanuel Kant is based on the Wikipedia entry on Kant (July, 2008), Churchman (1971), and Mason and Mitroff (1973).

5 The Hegelian view and information politics

1 This description of Hegel is based on the Wikipedia page on Hegel and especially Churchman's (1971) description. A more detailed account can be found in Redding (2006).
2 The Wikipedia page, however, states that Hegel used this classification only once, and he attributed the terminology to Immanuel Kant. Instead of "thesis–antithesis–synthesis," Hegel used different terms to speak about triads, for example "immediate–mediate–concrete," as

well as "abstract–negative–concrete." Hegel's work speaks of synthetic logic. Believing that the traditional description of Hegel's philosophy in terms of thesis–antithesis–synthesis was mistaken, a few scholars, like Raya Dunayevskaya, have attempted to discard the triadic approach altogether. Mason and Mitroff (1973: 481), though, recognize an interesting difference in Kant's and Hegel's work regarding dialects. Kant used the term to denote a logic of detecting multiple perspectives and ways of finding complementarity among these insights. Hegel sees theses and antitheses as real conflicts of opinion.

3 For an interesting classical story on information politics within organizations outside the context of the Internet, see Markus (1983).

4 As an estimate, we may use the number of Internet pages indexed by the Google search engine, which passed 1 trillion in July 2008. Source: http://googleblog.blogspot.com/2008/07/we-knew-web-was-big.html. Each page may contain several documents, and Google's coverage of the Internet is not 100 percent, as we will discuss shortly in this chapter.

5 Source: http://blog.searchenginewatch.com/blog/050123-123438.

7 The Singerian view and information management research

1 With regard, though, to this simplistic optimism, Churchman notes that it is doubtful whether Singer himself would so strongly express his hope for mankind.

References

Albert, T., Goes, P., and Gupta, A. (2004) "GIST: A model for design and management of content and interactivity of customer-centric web sites," *Management Information Systems Quarterly*, 28(2): 161–182.

Barnard, C. (1938) *The Functions of the Executive.* Cambridge, MA: Harvard University Press.

Becker, J., Delfmann, P., and Knackstedt, R. (2007a) "Adaptive reference modeling: Integrating configurative and generic adaptation techniques for information models," in J. Becker and P. Delfmann (eds.) *Proceedings of the 10th Workshop on Reference Modeling*, Berlin, pp. 23–49.

Becker, J., Pfeiffer, D., and Räckers, M. (2007b) "Domain specific process modelling in public administrations—The PICTURE-Approach," in *Proceedings of the Sixth International EGOV Conference (LNCS 4656)*, Regensburg, pp. 68–79.

Beer, S. (1985) *Diagnosing the system for organizations.* Chichester: Wiley.

Berenson, A. (2003) *The Number: How the Drive for Quarterly Earnings Corrupted Wall Street and Corporate America.* New York: Random House.

Bharadwaj, A., Sambamurthy, V., and Zmud, R. (1999) "IT capabilities: Theoretical perspectives and empirical operationalization," in *Proceedings of the 20th International Conference on Information Systems*, Charlotte, North Carolina, pp. 378–385.

Bhattacherjee, A. and Premkumar, G. (2004) "Understanding changes in belief and attitude toward information technology usage: A theoretical model and longitudinal test," *Management Information Systems Quarterly*, 28(2): 229–254.

Binney, D. (2001) "The knowledge management spectrum," *Journal of Knowledge Management*, 5(1): 33–42.

Bourhis, A., Dube, L., and Jacob, R. (2005) "The success of virtual communities of practice: The leadership factor," *The Electronic Journal of Knowledge Management*, 3(1): 23–34.

Burrell, G. and Morgan, G. (1979) *Sociological Paradigms and Organizational Analysis: Elements of the Sociology of Corporate Life.* London: Heineman.

Churchman, C. W. (1971) *The Design of Inquiring Systems: Basic Concepts of Systems and Organization.* New York: Basic Books.

Courtney, J. (2001) "Decision making and knowledge management in inquiring organizations: Toward a new decision-making paradigm for DSS," *Decision Support Systems,* 31: 17–38.

Dasselaar, A. (2004) *Handboek Internetresearch* (in Dutch). Netherlands: Van Duren Media.

Davenport, T. (1998) "Putting the enterprise into the enterprise system," *Harvard Business Review,* July/August: 121–133.

Denzin, N. (1970) *The Research Act: A Theoretical Introduction into Sociological Methods.* Chicago: Aldin.

Dietz, J. (2004) "Towards a LAP-based information paradigm," in M. Aakhus and M. Linds (eds.) *Proceedings of the 9th International Working Conference on the Language-Action Perspective on Communication Modeling.* New Brunswick, NJ: School of Communication, Information, and Library Studies, Rutgers, The State University of New Jersey, pp. 59–75.

Doll, W. and Torkzadeh, G. (1988) "The measurement of end-user computing satisfaction," *Management Information Systems Quarterly,* 12(2): 258–275.

Earl, M. (ed) (1996) *Information management: The organizational dimension.* Oxford: Oxford University Press.

Earl, M. (2001) "Knowledge management strategies: Toward a taxonomy," *Journal of Management Information Systems,* 18(1): 215–233.

Floridi, L. (2005) "Is semantic information meaningful data?," *Philosophy and Phenomenological Research,* 70(2): 351–370.

Floridi, L. (2007) "Semantic conceptions of information," in E. N. Zalta (ed.) *The Stanford Encyclopedia of Philosophy* (Spring 2007 Edition), http://plato.stanford.edu/archives/spr2007/entries/information-semantic.

Gasson, S. and Holland, N. (1995) "The nature and processes of IT-related change," in *Information Technology and Changes in Organizational Work. Proceedings IFIP WG 8.2 Working Conference.* London: Chapman & Hall, pp. 213–234.

George, C. (1972) *The History of Management Thought.* Englewood Cliffs, NJ: Prentice Hall.

Gilad, B. and Gilad, T. (1988) *The Business Intelligence System.* Boston, MA: AMACOM.

Gordijn, J. and Akkermans, H. (2001) "Designing and evaluating e-business models," *IEEE Intelligent Systems,* 16(4): 11–17.

Green, P. and Rosemann, M. (2000) "Integrated process modeling: An ontological evaluation," *Information Systems,* 25(2): 73–87.

Gregor, S. (2006) "The nature of theory in information systems," *Management Information Systems Quarterly,* 30(3): 611–642.

Guetzkow, H. (1965) "Communication in organizations," in J. March (ed.) *Handbook of Organizations*, Chicago, IL: Rand McNally, pp. 534–573.

Hammer, M. and Champy, J. (2003) *Reengineering the Corporation: A Manifesto for Business Revolution*. New York: Harper Business Essentials (first printed 1993).

Hammond, J., Keeny, R., and Raiffa, H. (1999) *Smart Choices—A Practical Guide to Making Better Life Decisions*. Boston, MA: Harvard Business School Press.

Hansen, M., Nohria, N., and Tierney, T. (1999) "What's your strategy for knowledge management?," *Harvard Business Review*, 77(2): 106–166.

Hedman, J. and Kalling, Th. (2003) "The business model concept: Theoretical underpinnings and empirical illustration," *European Journal of Information Systems*, 12: 49–59.

Hevner, A., March, S., and Ram, S. (2004) "Design science in information systems research," *Management Information Systems Quarterly*, 28(1): 75–105.

Hoffer, J. A., Prescott, M. B, and McFadden, F. R. (2002) *Modern Database Management*. Upper Saddle River, NJ: Prentice Hall.

Hofstede, G. (1981) "Management control of public and not-for-profit activities," *Accounting, Organizations and Society*, 6(3): 193–211.

Iivari, J., Hirschheim, R., and Klein, H. (2000) "A dynamic framework for classifying information systems development methodologies and approaches," *Journal of Management Information Systems*, 17(3): 179–218.

Jonkers, H., Lankhorst, M., Van Buuren, R., Hoppenbrouwers, S., Bonsangue, M., and Van der Torre, L. (2004) "Concepts for modelling enterprise architectures," *International Journal of Cooperative Information Systems*, 13(3): 257–287.

Jonscher, C. (1994) "An economic study of the information technology," in T. J. Allen, and M. S. Scott Morton (Eds.) *Information Technology and the Corporation of the 1990s*, New York: Oxford University Press, pp. 5–42.

Kambil, A. and Van Heck, E. (1998) "Reengineering the Dutch flower auctions: A framework for analyzing exchange organizations," *Information Systems Research*, 9(1): 1–19.

Kant, I. (1781) *Critique of Pure Reason*. Translated from German by Meiklejohn, J. http://gutenberg.org/etext/4280.

Kaplan, R. and Norton, D. (1996) *The Balanced Scorecard: Translating Strategy into Action*. Boston, MA: Harvard Business School Press.

Keck, O. (1987) "The information dilemma: Private information as a cause of transaction failure in markets, regulation, hierarchy, and politics," *The Journal of Conflict Resolution*, 31(1): 139–163.

Kerr, R. (1990) *Knowledge-Based Manufacturing Management: Applications of Artificial Intelligence to the Effective Management of Manufacturing Companies*. Boston, MA: Addison-Wesley.

Kienholz, A., Hayes, P., Mishra, R., and Engel, J. (1993) "Further validation of the Revised Inquiry Mode Questionnaire," *Psychological Reports*, 72(1): 779–784.

Kingston, J. and MacIntosh, A. (2000) "Knowledge management through multi-perspective modeling: Representing and distributing organizational memory," *Knowledge-Based Systems*, 13: 121–131.

Kirch, W. and Klein, H-K. (1977) *Management Informationssysteme*. Mainz: Kohlhammer.

Klein, H. and Myers, M. (1999) "A set of principles for conducting and evaluating interpretive field studies in information systems," *MIS Quarterly*, 23(1): 67–94.

Kling, R. (1980) "Social aspects of computing: Theoretical perspectives in recent empirical research," *Computing Surveys*, 12: 61–110.

Klir, G. and Yuan, B. (1995) *Fuzzy Sets and Fuzzy Logic: Theory and Applications*. Upper Saddle River, NJ: Prentice Hall.

Kolb, D. (1984) *Experiential Learning: Experience as the Source of Learning and Development*. Englewood Cliffs, NJ: Prentice Hall.

Kroenke, D. (2008) *Experiencing Management Information Systems*. Upper Saddle River, NJ: Pearson Prentice Hall.

Kuhn, Th. (1970) *The Structure of Scientific Revolutions*. Chicago, IL: University of Chicago Press, second edition.

Kumar, K. (1990) "Post implementation evaluation of computer-based information systems: Current practices," *Communications of the ACM*, 33(2): 203–212.

Landau, M. (1969) "Redundancy, rationality and the problem of duplication and overlap," *Public Administration Review*, 29(4): 346–358.

Lawrence, S. and Giles, L. (1999) "Accessibility of information on the web," *Nature*, 400: 107–109.

Look, B. C. (2008) "Gottfried Wilhelm Leibniz", in E. N. Zalta (ed.) *The Stanford Encyclopedia of Philosophy* (Spring 2008 Edition), http://plato.stanford.edu/archives/spr2008/entries/leibniz.

Lucas, H. C. (1996) *The T-Form Organization: Using Information Technology to Design Organizations for the 21st Century*. San Francisco: Jossey Bass.

Luftman, J., Kempaiah, M., and Nash, E. (2006) "Key issues for IT executives 2005," *Management Information Systems Quarterly Executive*, 5(2): 81–99.

MacKie-Mason, J., Shenker, S., and Varian, H. (1996) "Service architecture and content provision: The network provider as editor," *Telecommunications Policy*, 20(3): 203–218.

Markus, M. L. (1983) Power, politics, and MIS implementation. *Communications of the ACM*, 26(6): 430–444.

Markus, M. L. (1984) *Systems in Organizations: Bugs and Features*. Boston, MA: Pitman.

Markus, M., Majchrzak, A., and Gasser, L. (2002) "A design theory for systems that support emergent knowledge processes," *Management Information Systems Quarterly*, 26(3): 179–212.

Martin, L. (1986) "Eskimo words for snow: A case study in the genesis and decay of an anthropological example," *American Anthropologist*, 88(2): 418–423.

Mason, R. and Mitroff, I. (1973) "A program for research on management information systems," *Management Science*, 19(5): 475–487.

Mingers, J. (2001) "Combining IS research methods: Towards a pluralist methodology," *Information Systems Research*, 12(3): 240–259.

Mingers, J. (2008) "Management knowledge and knowledge management: Realism and forms of truth," *Knowledge Research and Practice*, 6: 62–76.

Moore, G. (1965) *Cramming more components onto electronic circuits.* Electronics 38 (8).

Mintzberg, H. (1983) *Structures in Fives: Designing Effective Organizations.* Englewood Cliffs, NJ: Prentice Hall.

Nijssen, G. and Halpin, T. (1989) *Conceptual Schema and Relational Database Design: A Fact Oriented Approach.* New York: Prentice Hall.

Nonaka, I. (1994) "A dynamic theory of organizational knowledge creation," *Organization Science*, 5(1): 14–37.

Orlikowski, W. (1992) "The duality of technology: Rethinking the concept of technology in organizations," *Organization Science*, 3(3): 398–427.

Palmer, J. (2001) "Web site usability, design, and performance metrics," *Information Systems Research*, 13(2): 151–167.

Philippidou, S., Soderquist, K., and Prastacos, G. (2004) "Towards new public management in Greek public organizations: Leadership vs. management, and the path to implementation," *Public Organization Review*, 4(4): 317–337.

Picot, A. and Bortenlanger Heiner, C. (1997) "Organization of electronic markets: Contributions from the new institutional economics," *The Information Society*, 13(1): 107–123.

Popper, K. (1959) *The Logic of Scientific Discovery.* New York: Basic Books.

Rayport, J. F. and Sviokla, J. (1994) "Managing in the marketspace," *Harvard Business Review*, 72, November–December: 141–150.

Redding, P. (2006) "Georg Wilhelm Friedrich Hegel," in E. N. Zalta (ed.) *The Stanford Encyclopedia of Philosophy* (Fall 2006 Edition), http://plato.stanford.edu/archives/fall2006/entries/hegel.

Scheer, A. (1998) *Aris: Business Process Frameworks.* Heidelberg, Germany: Springer.

Shapiro, C. and Varian, H. (1999) *Information rules: A strategic guide to the network economy.* Boston (MA): Harvard Business School Press.

Soh, C. and Markus, M. (1995) "How IT creates business value: A process theory synthesis," in *Proceedings of the Sixteenth International Conference on Information Systems*, pp. 29–41.

Sowa, J. and Zachman, J. (1992) "Extending and formalizing the framework for information systems architecture," *IBM Systems Journal*, 31(3): 590–616.

Spenser, C. (2007) "Drawing on your knowledge with VisiRule," *IEEE Potentials*, Jan./Feb.: 20–25.

Stabell, C. and Fjeldsted, O. (1998) "Configuring value for competitive advantage: On chains, shops, and networks," *Strategic Management Journal*, 19: 413–437.

Stamper, R. (1973) *Information in Business and Administrative Systems*. New York: Wiley.

Stein, E. W. and Zwass, V. (1995) "Actualizing organizational memory with information systems," *Information Systems Research*, 6(2): 85–117.

Taylor, F. (1911) *The Principle of Scientific Management*. New York: Harper & Sons.

Tennent, J and Friend, G. (2005) *Guide to Business Modeling*. London: Profile Books.

Uzgalis, W. (2007) "John Locke," in E. N. Zalta (ed.) *The Stanford Encyclopedia of Philosophy* (Summer 2007 Edition), http://plato.stanford.edu/archives/sum2007/entries/locke.

Van der Zee, J. and De Jong, B. (1999) "Alignment is not enough," *Journal of Management Information Systems*, 16(2): 137–156.

Venkatraman, N. and Henderson, J. (1998) "Real strategies for virtual organizing," *Sloan Management Review*, Fall: 33–48.

Voermans, K. (2007) *Economic Validation of a Media Levy for Digital Music*. MSc thesis. Enschede: University of Twente.

Walls, J., Widmeyer, G., and El Sawy, O. (1992) "Building an information system design theory for vigilant EIS," *Information Systems Research*, 3(1): 36–59.

Walsham, G. (2005) "Learning about being critical," *Information Systems Journal*, 15(2): 111–117.

Watkins, E. (2007) "Kant's philosophy of science," in E. N. Zalta (ed.) *The Stanford Encyclopedia of Philosophy* (Winter 2007 Edition), http://plato.stanford.edu/archives/win2007/entries/kant-science.

Webster, J. and Watson, R. (2002) "Analyzing the past to prepare for the future: Writing a literature review," *Management Information Systems Quarterly*, 26(2): XIII–XXIII.

Weick, K. E. (1979) *The Social Psychology of Organizing*, second edition. New York: Random House.

Weill, P. and Broadbent, M. (2000) "Managing IT infrastructure: A strategic choice," in R. W. Zmud (ed.) *Framing the Domains of IT Management: Projecting the Future . . . Through the Past*. Cincinnati, OH: Pinnaflex.

Wigand, R. (1997) "Electronic commerce: Definition, theory, and context," *The Information Society*, 13(1): 1–16.

Wijnhoven, F. and Kraaijenbrink, J. (2008) "Product-oriented design theory for digital information services: A literature review," *Internet Research*, 18(1): 93–120.

Wilensky, H. (1967) *Organizational Intelligence: Knowledge and policy in government and industry*. New York: Basic Books.

Womack, R. (2002) Information intermediaries and optimal information distribution, *Library and Information Science Research*, 24(2): 129–155.

Yang, Z., Chai, S., Zhou, Z and Zhou, N. (2005) Development and validation of an instrument to measure user perceived service quality of information presenting Web portals, *Information & management* (42): 575–589.

Index

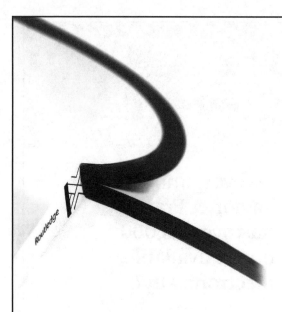